People Management
secrets

The experts tell all!

About the author

Rus Slater is a management consultant and trainer in the UK who has worked in many areas of industry, commerce and public service. He has managed people and advised on the management of teams for many years. He is the author of *Getting Things Done* and *Team Management*, also in the **business secrets** series.

Author's note

This book is dedicated to Caroline Jane Slater.

People Management
secrets

Collins

A division of HarperCollins*Publishers*

77-85 Fulham Palace Road, London W6 8JB

www.BusinessSecrets.net

First published in Great Britain in 2010 by HarperCollins*Publishers*
Published in Canada by HarperCollins*Canada*. www.harpercollins.ca
Published in Australia by HarperCollins*Australia*. www.harpercollins.com.au
Published in India by HarperCollins*PublishersIndia*. www.harpercollins.co.in

4

Copyright © HarperCollins*Publishers* 2010

SECRETS and BUSINESS SECRETS are trademarks of HarperCollins*Publishers*

Rus Slater asserts the moral right to be identified as the author of this work.

A catalogue record for this book is available from the British Library.

ISBN 978-0-00-734678-3

Printed and bound at Clays Ltd, St Ives plc

CONDITIONS OF SALE
This book is sold subject to the condition that it shall not, by way of trade or otherwise, be lent, re-sold, hired out or otherwise circulated without the publisher's prior consent in any form of binding or cover other than that in which it is published and without a similar condition including this condition being imposed on the subsequent purchaser.

All rights reserved. No part of this publication may be reproduced, stored in a retrieval system, or transmitted, in any form or by any means, electronic, mechanical, photocopying, recording or otherwise, without the prior permission of the publishers.

Mixed Sources
Product group from well-managed
forests and other controlled sources
www.fsc.org Cert no. SW-COC-001806
© 1996 Forest Stewardship Council

FSC is a non-profit international organisation established to promote the
responsible management of the world's forests. Products carrying the FSC
label are independently certified to assure consumers that they come
from forests that are managed to meet the social, economic and
ecological needs of present and future generations.

Find out more about HarperCollins and the environment at
www.harpercollins.co.uk/green

Contents

Introduction   8

1 Build a strong foundation   **10**
1.1 Know what your own boss expects   12
1.2 Decide if you are a manager or a leader   14
1.3 Balance your decisions   16
1.4 Don't be consistent!   18
1.5 Learn to delegate   20
1.6 Lead by example   22
1.7 Think about TOM   24
1.8 Create a ROWE   26

2 Create a great team   **28**
2.1 AIM to pick the right people for the job   30
2.2 Get the team performing quickly   32
2.3 Create a team identity   34
2.4 Create a team charter   36
2.5 Manage the people you don't see   38
2.6 Manage part-timers and
     matrix workers   40

3 Set goals and targets   **42**
3.1 Make proper plans   44
3.2 Define meaningful goals   46

3.3 Understand SMART goals   48
3.4 SMART is specific   50
3.5 SMART is measurable   52
3.6 SMART is achievable   54
3.7 SMART is relevant   56
3.8 SMART is time-bound   58
3.9 Know the SHABBY and PRISM
     approaches   60
3.10 Make the mundane more exciting   62

4 Motivate yourself and your people 64
4.1 Know the hierarchy of needs   66
4.2 Motivate beyond money   68
4.3 Identify people's personal motivators   70
4.4 Influence people to want
     what you want   72
4.5 'Catch' people doing things right   74
4.6 Empower your people   76
4.7 Practise the art of delegating   78
4.8 Support your people   80

5 Manage good performance   82
5.1 Identify good performance   84
5.2 Reward good performance   86
5.3 Help people learn from
     good performance   88

5.4	Maintain good performance in a crisis	90
5.5	Beware the 'Peter Principle'	92
6	**Manage poor performance**	**94**
6.1	Identify poor performance	96
6.2	Confront an instance of poor performance	98
6.3	Coach a poor performer to improve	100
6.4	Monitor a poor performer	102
6.5	'Manage out' a very poor performer	104
6.6	Analyse your own performance	106
7	**Develop your people**	**108**
7.1	Commit to developing your people	110
7.2	Develop people on a tight budget	112
7.3	Help people leave their 'comfort zones'	114
7.4	Set objectives that stretch people	116
7.5	Remember to develop yourself	118
7.6	Improve the working environment	120
7.7	Promote your people's image	122
	Jargon buster	124
	Further reading	126

Managing people is hard but rewarding

As you go through life, you will increasingly find that you need to manage people. A parent has to manage their family; a supervisor or team leader has to manage a small team; an entrepreneur may have to manage staff, customers and suppliers.

Early in my career I took responsibility for managing people. I managed up to 250 highly trained professionals who worked as a tight-knit team. It didn't matter that I was the youngest person in the team! For over 20 years I've been working with individuals and organizations to help them improve their management of people. This has ranged from military personnel to entrepreneurs, from charities to government departments. I've learned many secrets and tricks over these years. Some I've discovered for myself, but many I've learned from others. Humans are wonderfully inventive!

This book aims to help you improve your skills at managing people – to help you find ways in which everybody benefits. It contains 50 **secrets**, grouped into seven themed chapters.

■ **Build on a strong foundation.** You must understand what type of leader or manager you want to be. Your employer may give guidelines, but you must exert control over your day-to-day behaviour.

■ **Create a great team.** This shows how to choose the right people and quickly build a functioning team.

■ **Set goals and targets.** By setting people effective targets and goals, you can monitor progress and offer appropriate rewards.

■ **Motivate yourself and your people.** Implementing ways to motivate people is ultimately much easier than having to cajole and constantly monitor unmotivated people.

■ **Manage good performance.** You need to recognize good performance – reward it, develop it, perpetuate it and spread it to others. Otherwise you will lose your good performers and be left only with the poor ones.

■ **Manage poor performance.** Some managers find ways of managing *around* poor performance without tackling the poor performance itself. However, this encourages more poor performance, from both the original perpetrator and everyone else. Know how to tackle the problems head on.

■ **Develop your people.** Though often overlooked by managers, another fundamental task is developing people. You need to improve the less able, stretch and reward the able, plan succession for the future and mentor your people's changing needs.

Managing people is a hugely complex area in which you never stop learning. The **secrets** contained in this book will help you make massive strides towards succeeding in this fascinating role.

Knowing how to manage people well is one of the most important skills in life.

Build a strong foundation

A strong foundation is essential for anything you build, and this should include your management career. You need to decide from the outset if people will want to follow you or if you will be relying on the authority vested in you by your employer. How you act as manager will set a tone to be copied, loved, hated, criticized, praised or ignored. Be prepared to take the time to promote stability and longevity for your life in management.

1.1

Know what your own boss expects

You need to understand in detail what your own boss expects of you as a manager. Armed with this information, you can draw up specific targets for both yourself and your individual team members, and be confident in your day-to-day decision-making.

1 **Who is your boss?** If you work in a company or hierarchical structure, then there is usually a clear answer to this question – your boss is the person who appointed you or to whom you report. If you are an entrepreneur running your own business, however, your ultimate 'boss' may be the customer, or possibly your major shareholder or even the bank manager who allows

case study A sales manager had been set sales targets for him and his team to achieve. He was also set a target for cost reduction within the department and was required to ensure all his staff were trained to use the new software systems the organization introduced. As part of the organization's expansion plans,

you credit! If you work for a charity you need to be clear whether the 'boss' is the donor of the funds or the recipient of the benefit.

2 **What does your boss want?** If your boss is clear and concise about his or her wants, then you are able to move straight to setting targets for your people. If not, you are going to have to ask, and if necessary keep asking, until you get clear and SMART (see Secret 3.3) objectives.

3 **When does your boss want it?** Your boss will inevitably want you to achieve a number of different things, and you need to know the comparative priorities – what is most important/urgent and what is less so.

4 **How does your boss want it done?** This may include the detail of the method, but perhaps more importantly, the framework or environment in which it is to be done. For instance, are you constrained by quality procedures? Are there internal policies on health and safety, equality laws or human rights issues?

If you don't know your boss's expectations, then achieving them will be purely a matter of chance.

he was also tasked to investigate new markets and recruit new sales staff to exploit these. Unsure of priorities, he tried to achieve everything as soon as possible. After nine months he collapsed with exhaustion, having reached none of his targets or objectives in full. His team were branded as failures and dispersed.

1.2

Decide if you are a manager or a leader

Are you a manager or a leader? This is not about your job title. 'Leaders' have their 'followers', whereas 'managers' have 'the managed'. This may seem like a purely semantic difference, but there are different concepts behind the words.

■ **Followers.** These people actively choose to follow you. They want to support you, they want to work for you, and they want you to succeed, because your success proves they were right to follow you.

■ **The managed.** These people are relatively passive in working for you. They are happy to let you make all their decisions for them. They do as they are told and leave it up to you to check the quality of their work. They don't try to use their initiative because they believe that is what *you* are paid for. They give you the 'right to manage'.

one minute wonder There is a quote from a staff members' annual report that reads: "This person is capable of producing adequate results when under constant supervision and when caught like a rat in a trap!" Does this describe any of your own people?

Followers require less:	Followers require more:	The managed require more:
Supervision	Respect	Instructions
Checking up on	Empowerment	Complete/comprehensive instructions
Monitoring	Trust	Frequent supervision
Chasing	Freedom to improve processes	Protection from simple distractions
Handholding	Protection from interference	Management thinking on their behalf
Helping	Freedom to manage own workload and goals	Quality control

It is probably pretty clear that your life will be more fulfilling and more enjoyable if you are a leader than a manager, but pressure (target-driven organizations, the desire to be indispensable, the feeling of responsibility) tends to encourage micro-management.

You probably need to 'manage' people who have little experience and expertise, but as people grow in ability and knowledge you can slowly switch from 'manager' to 'leader'. Of course, if you take over a team that is already performing, you may be able to go straight to leadership and followership from day one.

A leader attracts followers, whereas a manager has to supervise the managed.

1.3

Balance your decisions

Are you the leader of the team, or the person tasked to get things done, or the person tasked with looking after the individual team members? Actually, if you want to manage people well, you need to take on all three of these roles.

There is a concept called 'Pyrrhic Victory', which describes a situation in which an objective has been achieved – but at too high a cost.

■ If you make all decisions with the primary objective of achieving the task at any cost, then you might end up destroying the team on the way. But…
■ If you make all your decisions with the primary aim of keeping the team intact and happy, then you probably won't achieve the task. But…
■ If you are determined to ensure that each and every individual is safe, happy and looked after, then you won't fulfil the task and the team will fall apart as well.

John Adair, the world's first Professor of Leadership Studies, developed a model called Action Centred Leadership. His contention is that as a leader or manager you need to ensure that every decision and action you take balances the needs of the task, the team and the individuals. By doing this you stand the greatest chance of achieving the task, having a cohesive and capable team still in place for the next task, and having individuals who still have a good quality of life, and feel valued and respected.

This model is usually represented by three interlocking circles, from which it gets its name, Action *Centred* Leadership.

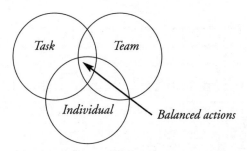

Task considerations	Team considerations	Individual considerations
Will this action: ■ Define the task? ■ Get the task completed? ■ Achieve the quality standard required? ■ Solve problems that will otherwise stop the task from being completed?	Will this action: ■ Support the team as a whole? ■ Spread workloads effectively? ■ Keep team members informed about team issues? ■ Encourage communication within the team?	Will this action: ■ Favour any one individual? ■ Exclude any individual? ■ Overload any individual? ■ Develop individuals' weaknesses? ■ Work to individuals' strengths?

Answering yes or no to any of the questions above doesn't tell you the right thing to do. By asking the questions before you act, you will get a chance to balance your decision.

Balanced decisions every day make for good leadership – not task focused one day, team focused the next!

1.4

Don't be consistent!

"What?" I hear you cry! "Surely I should manage everyone in the same way to be fair?" Well, think about it: imagine you have two people, one is experienced, competent and willing, and the other is new to the task, has little ability and is lazy. Would it be fair to manage each of them in the same way? Would it motivate them both?

You have to manage or lead in a way that suits the situation. This is called Situational Leadership, a title originally coined by Ken Blanchard and Paul Hersey. Here is a simple primer to the idea:

■ Consider an individual's *ability* on a scale of low to high. This is their ability to do the job you are asking of them, not just a reflection of their age or years of service.

■ Next consider their *willingness* to do this particular job, again on a scale of low to high.

■ Now imagine these two values plotted on a graph, like the one opposite.

■ The notations on the graph (C, D1, D2, S) refer to the paragraphs below the graph, which tell you how you might best manage this particular person.

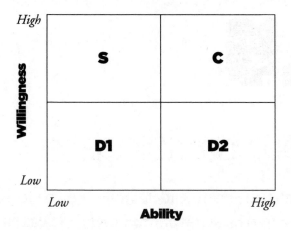

■ **S = Support.** This person is very willing but lacking in skill/ability. They need support in terms of demonstrations, training and practice (see Secret 4.8).

■ **C = Coaching.** This person is both willing and able and therefore only needs some light coaching in order to perform well.

■ **D1 = Directing 1.** This person has both low ability and low willingness. They are going to need much more in the way of directing – orders, supervision and checking.

■ **D2 = Directing 2.** This person has already proved their ability but their willingness is low. They don't need training and demonstration; they need some direction from you to understand why the task is important and how they will benefit personally by doing it well.

It is vital for your success and the success of your people that you manage in a way that suits the situation.

1.5

Learn to delegate

As a manager, team leader, supervisor or foreman, you have to delegate work to others. Delegating is a fundamental skill of management, but it is also one that many managers do very badly. There is a skill to learn in order to delegate effectively.

The more you delegate, the more time you will have to manage people and improve processes. In order to delegate effectively, you need to ensure that the person to whom you delegate a task is provided with four things: Skill, Time, Authority and Responsibility. The first letters of these words spell the word **STAR**, which makes them easy to remember, as shown below.

■ **S = Skill.** You need to ensure that the person has the skill and ability to do the task. This doesn't mean that they have to be as good at the task as you. (You may be able to give them more time to do it than you would otherwise have available to do it yourself.)

■ **T = Time.** You need to make sure that the person has adequate time to complete the task at the pace that's likely for their ability. This means allowing for the actual time this task will take alongside any other tasks they need to do. If you are their manager, they may be reluctant to admit that they don't have the time. Try to ask open questions ("When will you do this?") rather than leading questions ("You have enough time to do this, don't you?") to ascertain their workload.

■ **A = Authority.** Ensure that other people know that the person you're delegating to has been given the authority to complete this task. You might just tell people that they will need to provide this person with information and support, or you might give them a written 'licence' or acting rank. Without confirmation of authority, their task may be much harder to perform.

■ **R = Responsibility.** This is often the hardest one. You are delegating something that you have a responsibility to get done, so you must ensure that the person you delegate to understands that they are *responsible to you* for doing the task. One of the best ways to give the responsibility is to make it very clear that you are sharing the credit for the successful outcome.

For more about delegating to motivate people, see Secret 4.7.

The more you can delegate properly the more you can get done, so learn to love delegating.

1.6

Lead by example

We have already established that it is easier for you if your people want to follow you rather than be 'the managed'. You have to set a good example for people to copy. Otherwise, you are giving the contradictory message, "Don't do as I do, do as I say."

■ Leading by example *doesn't mean* that you have to do or even be able to do the jobs of everyone who works for you.

■ Leading by example *doesn't mean* that you have to get as 'grimy' as they may have to on a daily basis.

■ Leading by example *doesn't mean* that you have to earn the same as they do. The extra responsibilities of being the boss usually command a higher rate of pay.

one minute wonder The difficult balancing act is to let people see that you have achieved your elevated position on merit, without making them resent you for the trappings of that achievement. If you can get this balance right, then you are a leader!

If you expect your people to be able to work unsupervised…	…you must let them work unsupervised.
If you expect them to respect you…	…you have to respect them.
If you want them to listen to you…	…you must be prepared to listen to them.
If you want their opinions…	…you must ask for their opinions.
If you expect them to work contracted hours…	…you must be seen to work contracted hours.
If you want them to fulfil tasks…	…don't set unfulfillable tasks.
If you want people to act with integrity and follow the rules…	…you must act with integrity and obey the rules.
If you want people to be pro-active and use initiative…	…you have to encourage and reward initiative.
If you want a happy, cheerful workplace…	…you have to be cheerful yourself.
If you want people to be positive, upbeat, enthusiastic and energetic…	…you have to demonstrate a generally positive attitude.

You have to set an example all day, every day. People really notice and remember if you fail to 'walk the talk'.

1.7

Think about TOM

TOM is an acronym. It sets out three simple to remember principles that help you manage people effectively. The three principles of TOM are Trust, Objectives and Motivation.

■ **Trust.** You need to build trust with your people. Note the emphasis on *trust with*, i.e. you trust them and they trust you. You can do this by observing, questioning, listening to and socializing with your people. Manage their expectations and keep your word. Always be reasonable. Building trust takes time, and you don't command trust just because of your rank or job title. Avoid 'micro-management' – don't expect hourly progress reports. Step back and let people get on without your constant supervision.

■ **Objectives.** You need to set objectives that have clear desired outcomes. These can be short-, medium- or long-term objectives. They can be based around activity and effort or results, as appropriate, so long as the way you will (and therefore the individual can) assess success is clearly understood. Chapter 3 covers the required elements of a good objective.

■ **Motivation.** You must ensure that the individual has adequate motivation. Recognize that sometimes the responsibility alone is motivation enough and that at other times it will not be. Like the objective, the motivation can be short or long term: "If you get all this filing done today, you can do the research you enjoy tomorrow. If you get all the research finished by the end of the day tomorrow, you can have Wednesday afternoon off!"

Business gurus who have successfully managed people in the real world agree with the TOM approach:

"If you pick the right people and give them the opportunity to spread their wings *[Trust]* and put compensation as a carrier behind it *[Motivation]* you almost don't have to manage them" *[just set the Objectives]*
Jack Welch, former Chairman and CEO of General Electric

"I have no secret. There are no rules to follow in business. I just work hard *[set and achieve Objectives]* and, as I always have done, believe I can do it. *[Trust myself]* Most of all, though, I try to have fun" *[Motivation]*
Sir Richard Branson, Chairman of Virgin Group

"Tell them what you want *[Objectives]*, reward them for it *[Motivation]*, and get out of the way" *[Trust]*
Gordon Bethune, former CEO of Continental Airlines

Agree objectives, check people are motivated and then get out of the way!

1.8

Create a ROWE

A Results Orientated Work Environment – or ROWE for short – is a new idea that is gaining ground in the information and Internet age. The main principle behind ROWE is to create a working environment that is orientated to recognizing and rewarding *results* rather than *time*.

In order to create a ROWE, the manager has to set specific, measurable objectives that lead to results that can be tested and accepted. (See Chapter 3 for more about setting objectives.) The key concept in a ROWE is the quality standard by which you, the manager, will assess whether the task has been completed, and therefore whether the reward for it will be released.

Obviously the faster a person can complete a task to the required standard, the sooner they earn the reward. This challenge in itself encourages people to work with a higher level of motivation.

ROWE doesn't work for all roles. For example, a shop assistant has to be present while the shop is open, even if there are no customers. However, for roles that can be done on a ROWE basis, the approach has distinct benefits.

one minute wonder Consider what you want the people who work for you to achieve... today... and this week. Does it really require them to be in the office, or is being in the office actually a hindrance to their achievement? If so... think ROWE!

■ People can manage their own workloads and don't need to ask your permission to come and go. Therefore you don't need to constantly supervise and monitor their work rate and attendance.
■ People can earn more if they want to, which is another motivating factor.
■ Reward is based on actual output, not hours, so productivity is very likely to rise.
■ ROWE increases everyone's focus on quality.
■ ROWE is an adaptive solution to overwork – people are less likely to take on work they do not intend to complete.

ROWE works best if the people you manage are not a team, and the output of each is independent of others. However, you can create a team ROWE – a team of bricklayers, for example, can agree a 'contract price' for the job. They will be far more reliable than a team of bricklayers paid by the hour who have, by definition, a vested interest in dragging out the job to take up more hours.

A work environment orientated to results has many benefits over one based on the number of hours worked.

Create a great team

If you have the opportunity, form your people into a team. Teams don't occur naturally; you have to make a concerted effort to develop a team ethos. This chapter is mostly concerned with creating a team from a group of individuals. The whole point of a team is 'synergy', which means that the whole is greater than the sum of the parts. In other words, teamwork will produce a better result than when individual people work towards individual goals.

2.1

AIM to pick the right person for the job

Managing people is a whole lot easier if you have the right people from the outset. If you have the opportunity to pick and choose your people, then this secret will help you to take advantage of that opportunity. There are three fundamental steps to picking the right people – Assess, Identify and Motivate – or AIM for short.

1 **Assess what 'right' is.** Analyse what you want this person to do and create a Job Description. What level of skills and knowledge do they need? For instance, does this person need to be 'familiar with' or 'expert with' Microsoft Office Tools? What personal attributes will they need to be successful and satisfied? If the team is working in an ever-changing environment, you will need a different type of person to someone who would suit a team whose predominant environment is bureaucratic and slow moving. What type of person will fit in with your style of management? If you like empowering people, someone who needs constant reassurance will be unhappy. What type of person

> **"Genius is the ability to pick the right person for the job and then let them get on with it"** Anonymous

will fit in with the other team members? This is tricky, because sometimes someone who is similar is best, and at other times someone who complements the other team members is best.

2 **Identify your options and identify the 'right' person.** Now you have to find some potential recruits. You can use the answers you came up with in section 1 above to draft an advertisement that helps people to know if they are qualified and whether the job is the type they'd want. Once you have some people to interview, you can again use the answers from section 1 to help you find and assess evidence of the person's competence to do what you need them to do.

3 **Motivate that person to want to join your team.** Once you have found the person you think is right, you have to 'sell' them the opportunity. Up until now you have been focusing on *your* needs, but now you need to focus on *their* needs. See Secret 4.3 to help you here.

You will notice that the three steps above – **Assess, Identify, Motivate** – spell out the word **AIM**. It is rather like throwing a basketball – if you AIM properly you will score!

Pick the right person for the job, and they will be a happy person, which in turn will make you a happy manager!

2.2

Get the team performing quickly

The 'Tuckman Model' identifies several stages that a team goes through before it starts performing properly. The stages – referred to as Forming, Storming, Norming and Performing – will happen naturally, but you can speed up the process.

1 **Forming stage.** Forming is the introduction process, when people are literally finding out who is who, learning names, job titles, roles and ranks, and other people's history. In order to get this stage successfully completed as quickly as possible, deliberately hold a 'forming' meeting. Ask everyone to introduce themselves and share this information.

case study A manager asked me to run a teambuilding course for his part-time IT project team. The team had spent 11 months and many thousands of pounds but had achieved nothing at all. Over two days of teambuilding, the team members properly introduced

2 **Storming stage.** The stage where, confident they are meant to be here, people start to 'jockey for position' – to establish their credibility in the team. Some will try to push themselves forward because they want power or influence; others will deliberately keep a low profile because they are shy, diffident or lacking in confidence. You need to set up activities that allow people to find their level of comfort – for example any of the teambuilding exercises you can find on websites such as www.businessballs.com.

3 **Norming stage.** This is when you start to establish the rules of behaviour between team members, and their relationships with you and people outside. The Norming phase can take quite a long time if left to happen naturally because the rules will be established by a combination of 'trial and error' and 'custom and practice'. Take control by holding a team meeting to set up a formal 'team charter'. See Secret 2.4 for more details.

4 **Performing stage.** Performing is the stage when the team is getting on with the tasks in hand. Milestones are reached, targets are met, internal friction is minimal, people are smiling and achieving.

Help your people get through the early stages of teambuilding quickly.

themselves to each other for the first time; they did a couple of exercises that allowed them to 'storm'; and they produced their own team charter. They went on to achieve more in the following six weeks than they had in the previous 11 months.

2.3

Create a team identity

Sports teams nearly always have a team name, whether it's British Lions (rugby union team), the Mumbai Champs (cricket team), the Tianjin Lions (baseball team) or the Mamelodi Sundowns (soccer team). Teams have names because it gives them a sense of being a team and it makes the members feel as if they 'belong'!

Even if the people on your team are scattered across several departments of the organization, they can work together happily if they have a sense of shared identity. You should create a team identity – a team name, a team logo, a team motto, a team vision and even a team 'strip' or uniform.

Get your team together and suggest the idea: they'll probably like it. You can ask them to work in pairs or small groups to select an appropriate name, devise a logo, think up a motto and design a 'uniform'. They can each present their suggestions to the rest of the team and you can have a vote for the most popular. Opposite are some guidelines you can give them.

■ **Team name.** Keep it short and simple, for example The 'Hey!' Team rather than the Global Internal Corporate Communications Team. Go for something descriptive of the team's role or style, such as The Paper Tigers for an archive team. Try to find something different or even unique. Whereas lots of organizations have a Quality Team, why not call it The DriFTers, standing for Do it Right First Time? Alliterative or punning names are usually successful – the Rajasthan Royals or Coach and Courses for your training team. Also make sure the name is easy to pronounce and spell in the language your team uses – a good example of a 'team' that adopted an easier name identity is the British Royal Family, who changed their surname from Saxe-Coburg-Gotha to Windsor in 1917.

■ **Team logo.** Keep the logo simple so that it stays recognizable when reduced in size on memos or polo shirts. Ideally, create one in black and white or primary colours so it can easily be photocopied and replicated if you want to have it embroidered, painted or printed. Look at famous logos like UPS, Chanel, Citroën, Nike, Puma, BMW or the BBC for inspiration – all use simple, strong shapes and colours.

■ **Team motto.** Keep it short and informative of the team ethos. Think about famous slogans such as Avis's *"We try Harder"*.

■ **Team 'uniform'.** You can create a team 'uniform' with clothing and accessories, such as hats, polo shirts, badges, buttons, umbrellas, document bags, and so on. Items such as these are all relatively cheap, unisex and often more popular and fun than a top-to-toe uniform.

Get your people involved in creating a team identity.

2.4

Create a team charter

In Secret 2.2 we looked at the Tuckman Model (Forming, Storming, Norming and Performing). The creation of a team charter will help you through the Storming and Norming phases, allowing people to get on with the business of Performing.

A team charter is a set of rules, or norms of behaviour, that clearly sets out the acceptable behaviour among members of the team (including you as the team leader). Depending on the circumstances, it might also set out acceptable behaviour to other 'stakeholders' – internal departments, customers, competitors, shareholders, patients and so on.

In order to cover both Storming and Norming phases, it is better to get the team to 'Storm' the 'Norms' and create the charter themselves rather than you imposing the rules upon the team. This may seem counter-intuitive, but you can lead the team to produce their Norms.

■ Get the team together, ideally away from the workplace but certainly somewhere where you can work without disturbance for a few hours.
■ Give everyone a pen and paper.
■ Ask each person to complete the following sentence: "I hope that X happens within this team." Ask them to do this alone, because you want individual answers, not the consensus, at this stage. People can write as many sentences as they want.

Typically the sort of answers you get will be: "That people will listen to me", "That people will tell the truth", "That everyone will work hard", "That credit will be given for success", and similar.

■ Write these answers onto a big flipchart sheet.
■ Now lead a discussion that relates to: "What must I do to make this hope a reality?" ("I" refers to each team member individually.) Make sure that you get the opinions of everyone in the team, not just the loudest or most senior. Make sure everyone is prepared to accept, abide by and support the wording of the 'Promise'.
■ As you complete each line, write in the 'Promises', as in the example below:

Hope	Promise
"That people will listen to me."	"I will say what I mean, at an appropriate time."
"That people will tell the truth."	"I will presume that people are telling the truth unless I have cause to believe otherwise."
"That everyone will work hard."	"I will work hard at my job and assist others where I can."

Once you have written up a Promise to go with each Hope, you will have created a team charter. It will be the outcome of the team Storming (under your guidance) and will reflect behaviour that everyone accepts and commits to.

Doing a team charter exercise with the whole team speeds you through the Storming and Norming phases.

2.5

Manage the people you don't see

In the modern world we increasingly find ourselves managing 'virtual teams', where some or even all of the team are based in different locations. This means that we don't see these people on a daily or even monthly basis. When this is the case, we have to work harder to make sure that the people are still our followers and we are still their leaders.

When your people are near to you, they see you every day and you see them. This makes it easier for you to catch people doing things 'right' (Secret 4.5) and for you to ensure that you are seen to be interested in the team and the individuals (Secret 1.3).

When some or all of your team are based somewhere else, you need to use all the technology available to you as well as really take the time to ensure that you still lead and manage these people.

Opposite are some things you can do to help you successfully manage the virtual team.

■ **Encourage feedback from the outset.** Teams skilled in giving and receiving feedback tend to do better in situations of working virtually. Therefore, taking time initially to go through the Forming and Storming stages of building your team (Secret 2.2) will pay dividends even more with a remote team.

■ **Establish common values.** Teams that establish common working values and standards stay more cohesive, so developing your team charter (secret 2.4) is also a powerful way to make it easier to manage a virtual team.

■ **Make an effort to meet.** You will need to devote more of your time to travelling to visit your remote team members or to setting up telephone conversations or conference calls to ensure that they are included in team briefings and regular feedback sessions.

■ **Communicate clearly.** Conciseness in communication is really important. Make sure that your personal communication style is succinct, accurate and not open to misinterpretation!

■ **Build up levels of trust.** Trust is even more important in virtual teams, as it is easier for a virtual team to fall apart through lack of trust.

■ **Set up the right communications technology.** The organization needs to provide good, simple systems for virtual communication.

Managing a virtual team is the same as managing a normal team, just harder!

2.6

Manage part-timers and matrix workers

Consider a national sports team: all the players are brought together to play for their country, but they also belong to a local team. When the national competition is over they go back to their local team. Does the national team manager manage them any less simply because they are part-timers?

Some, or even all, of your team may have other bosses within your organization. This means that they, and you, are only a 'part-time team'. For instance, you may be the Account Manager for a client account; in your team are two sales people who are also selling to other accounts; an operations administrator who looks after a region where other accounts are also active; four delivery drivers, each of whom covers other clients' deliveries on the same journeys; and you are all supported by an accounts clerk who is responsible for sales across the whole region.

Each of these people has another boss in the organization who demands their time, commitment and loyalty. To all intents and purposes, you are competing with those other bosses for your team members' support! However, you can minimize the problems of this 'matrix management' by taking the following actions.

one minute wonder Meet with each of the other managers of all your team members at the very beginning of the team's existence. Make sure that they know who you are and how to reach you to discuss any issues that may arise from the fact that their staff members are trying to serve two masters.

1 Build your team's vision and identity in the minds of your team members.

2 Be considerate but assertive regarding the conflicts of interest that your team members are having to juggle.

3 Form relationships with the other matrix managers to reduce the possibility of conflict.

4 Be very clear in your communications with team members and their matrix managers.

5 Liaise with matrix managers over matters of timekeeping, performance and performance appraisal.

6 Recognize that, if they have matrix managers, workers are likely to be a virtual team and therefore need more thoughtful management from you (see Secret 2.5).

Understand the potential conflicts of interest when your people work for other managers too.

Set goals and targets

When you set meaningful targets and goals, your people have something to strive for and know what is expected of them. Goal-setting allows you to monitor the progress of individuals and the team, which in turn allows you to reward accordingly. People who are seen to be achieving their targets and goals need less micro-management from you, and everyone will generally benefit.

3.1

Make proper plans

In an ever-changing world there is a strong likelihood that any plan will be superseded before it is executed. This leads to a temptation for some managers to avoid planning and try always to be flexible instead. However, a better approach is to make good plans and be open to changing them if need be.

A plan has a number of common elements, no matter what industry you are in and what level you are at. You need to work out the answers to the following questions in writing.

1 **Why does the plan exist?** In other words, define what it is you are attempting to achieve overall. This should clarify what successful achievement of the plan will look like.

2 **How are you proposing to achieve this?** Answer this in relatively 'big picture' terms. You can include a summary of the answers to the next three questions in the 'big picture'.

3 **Who is going to be involved?** This can range from names of people to names of departments and organizations.

"I love it when a plan comes together"

Hannibal Smith, character in 'The A-Team' TV series

4 **What are they going to be doing?** This is important so that everyone can see what everyone else is doing, which ensures that there is no unnecessary crossover and highlights areas that have been missed.

5 **When is the plan scheduled to be completed?** Initially this may simply be the end date of the overall plan, but as the plan is developed in more detail it may also contain the completion dates for milestones within the plan.

In the modern world we are usually under pressure (some of it self-generated) to "stop thinking/talking about it, and get on with it". Sadly this discourages us from spending time planning, which usually results in a false start that wastes time, energy and money.

Making a plan provides a range of benefits. For example, you know what you are doing day to day; your team knows what it's trying to achieve; each team member knows what his or her part is in the plan; you can use the plan to tell yourself and your boss of your commitments; the plan tells you what resources are needed; having a plan raises morale.

A detailed written plan proves to your team and your boss that you are thinking intelligently. Having spent the time in planning, you are less likely to be caught out by something you hadn't considered.

It is said that if you fail to plan, then you plan to fail!

3.2

Define meaningful goals

People work better when they are working towards a definite goal. As the team leader or manager, a large part of your job will be done if you set meaningful goals, both for the individual people on your team and for the team as a whole.

Getting meaningful goals from your boss

Unless you are an entrepreneur, then you need to be given meaningful goals by your boss before you can set goals for others. However, getting clear and concise goals from your boss is not always easy. He or she will, like you, be under a considerable degree of pressure and will have conflicting calls on his or her time.

If meaningful goals are not automatically given by your boss, then you will have to ask. You need to know your manager's overall expectations of you and your team for the next 12 months. Presuming that there will be more than one single objective, you need to know what the priorities are – what are the first quarter goals?

If you are unable to get an answer immediately, then ask again. This time point out that you don't want to disappoint your boss or waste a year of the organization's time.

one minute wonder You cannot set meaningful goals unless you get meaningful goals; therefore you may have to ask and challenge your boss in order to act like a good boss. This common scenario is part of the challenge of being a good manager of people!

If you still can't get your boss to offer a sensible set of goals, you should write a set of goals and priorities that seem appropriate. Take these to your boss and ask if they are acceptable. This, if nothing else, forces a debate about the direction your team should be taking.

Giving meaningful goals to your people

Once you have a set of goals and priorities for your team, you are able to start allocating individual goals and priorities for each team member. Remember that you don't want your people to disappoint you or waste a year, so you need to give each of them a personally meaningful set of goals and priorities.

When you have decided what you want each person to do, you need to have a discussion with each of them to ensure they accept that the goals are achievable. This isn't handing it over to a democracy, but a matter of ensuring that each person feels confident that they can, with your support, actually fulfil their goals. Whereas trying to do something that they resent because they don't think it is achievable is to head for disaster.

See also Secret 1.5 about delegation.

If you don't set meaningful goals for your people, who will? ("The devil makes work for idle hands!")

3.3

Understand SMART goals

When you set goals for people you need to ensure that the goal you set is not open to misinterpretation and provides as much appropriate detail as it can. To this end there is a mnemonic, SMART. This is a tried and trusted 'method' that is used (in one form or another) by numerous organizations in all sectors.

If you do an Internet search for 'SMART goal setting', you will find that even in English there is a wide range of interpretations for SMART, as different organizations develop the basic theory to fit their culture and circumstances. For the purposes of this Secret, and the five Secrets that follow we are going to say that **SMART** stands for:

■ **S = Specific.** This means that you need to make the goal as specific as possible. It is easy to be vague, but more useful for you (to appraise performance) and for the individual (to know what to do and how they are doing) to be clear and detailed about the goal. You don't have to tell them how to do it, but you should tell them exactly what you want it to look like at the end. Secret 3.4 contains more detail and examples.

■ **M = Measurable.** Measuring things is the way we take any subjectivity out of the future appraisal of whether the goal has been met. Usually by setting a measurement we are also able to assess the level of success achieved if the goal wasn't fully met. The difficulty is finding a suitable measure for many of the goals that we set. Secret 3.5 contains more detail and examples.

■ **A = Achievable.** This is a stumbling block for many managers. If a goal has to be accepted as achievable by the person undertaking it, doesn't that mean that people can simply refuse a goal and only agree something easy? The answer to this is no. The individual is able to argue the case that a specific goal is not achievable, but as the manager you have the final say. Secret 3.6 contains more detail and examples of achievable goals.

■ **R = Relevant.** Every goal you set has to be relevant to the overall purpose of the individual's job and the overall goal of the team. Secret 3.7 contains more detail and examples.

■ **T = Timebound.** Each individual goal you set will feed into the overall purpose and goal of the team. The team's goals will feed into the organization's goals. Consequently any goal achieved late has a knock-on effect. Therefore it is absolutely imperative that every goal is 'timebound' – people know when they are expected to deliver. Secret 3.8 contains more detail and examples.

SMART objectives can be expressed in a single sentence. For example: "My objective is to write 50 Secrets on the subject of People Management in MS Word format and submit them to the editor by close of business on the 15th of October."

SMART goals are set in organizations across the world. The next five secrets explain SMART factors in more detail.

3.4

SMART is specific

Most of us have a habit of presuming that when we communicate with other people, they understand exactly what we mean. However, the less specific we are, the less likely it is that other people will place the same interpretations on our words as we do.

If you ever find yourself giving an instruction like "get a grip", "sort it out", "take action now", "get rid of it" (or any other colloquialisms you might habitually use in your native parlance), you must stop and ask yourself whether the other people are likely to know what you mean by such instructions.

Similarly if you give someone a goal of "market the new product", do you mean "market" or "sell"? The two words have different meanings.

"Produce a report on", doesn't tell the person what the purpose of the report is. As a result, they don't know whether they are supposed to produce a report that compares, assesses, recommends or simply describes. "Take the visitors back to the airport" may be adequate if there is only one airport, it has only one terminal, the person knows how many visitors there are and how much luggage they have… if the recipient of this instruction isn't already armed with this information then the instruction is hopelessly non-specific.

"To choose well, you must know who you are and what you stand for, where you want to go and why you want to get there.**"** **Kofi Annan, UN Secretary-General (1997–2007)**

Here are some examples of specific goals:

■ Sell the product for a margin of $1.65.

■ Produce a report comparing the new product with the X product of the Y Company in terms of their specifications and price.

■ Take the four visitors to Terminal Three at Mumbai International airport for their flight back to the US.

■ Build a brick wall 1.8 metres high.

■ Learn to use MS Project in order to draw up a plan for Project X.

■ Make a profit of $45,000.

It is just as important to be specific about your annual goals as it is to be specific over the task for this afternoon.

Also note that a specific goal describes the output of the person's *action* rather than just the *activity* itself.

A specific goal is more likely to be achieved (to everyone's benefit) than a loose one.

3.5

SMART is measurable

'Measurable' is often synonymous with 'specific' but is not always the same, which is why it is a separate characteristic of a SMART objective. The primary point of the measurable aspect of a SMART objective is to give objectivity. It either is or isn't acceptable; it is not open to interpretation.

Measurable can be in almost any units (metres, feet, $, etc). It can be relative (% of improvement over the same quarter last year) or expressed in quality terms (to ISO 9001). It can also be expressed in negative terms in some instances ('error-free' for example).

one minute wonder Think about units of measurement in your industry. For example, customer satisfaction ratings can also be a measure for customer-facing staff and managers (internal customer satisfaction ratings can be a measure for support services). Staff retention or morale can be a measure for managers.

Examples of poor measurability

Objective	Comment
Improve sales of the X product line.	By how much? Is a 1% improvement acceptable?
Write a book on 'Managing People'.	How long should the book be? 20 pages or 500?
Write a 200-page book on 'Managing People'.	How many words is 200 pages? In font size 18 it will be about 80% the word count of font size 14.
Test run the repaired engine.	For how long, and at what operating temperature?

Examples of appropriate measurability

Objective	Comment
Increase sales of the X product line by 20% of units and 18% of revenue.	There are two measures in this example. These ensure that the product is not sold at loss-making prices in order to achieve a turnover target.
Write a user manual in clear American English that explains the position and function of all the controls of the vehicle. The manual is to be no more than 5 sides of A5 in typeface no smaller than 14 point.	There are two measures – clear American English and the size of the finished manual.
Machine a prototype drive shaft to the tolerances shown on the attached drawings.	The measurement is to a standard that is referred to in the stated objective.
Manage the reception desk effectively, ensuring that all cash and credit card receipts are authorized and accurate to invoices. Ensure that guests are never kept waiting more than 5 minutes.	This example contains three measures – authorized payments, accurate payments and customer waiting times.

Measurability removes subjectivity.

3.6

SMART is achievable

Nothing is more demoralizing than trying to do something that seems impossible. That is why the person who is taking on an objective has to agree that it is an achievable objective for them.

If you carefully consider the experience of the person and their full workload in the timescale given, then you should be able to propose an objective that you are confident is achievable.

Before giving this goal to the person, however, you could ask them to propose their own goal in line with the team goals. This will show you their level of confidence and commitment. If the goal falls far short of your own expectations, then you need to probe for the reasons behind this. You might identify a deficiency that you hadn't considered – lack of equipment, for example, or the fact that they will be unavailable for a week in the middle of the schedule. If no problems like that can be identified, then their reluctance to accept an objective that you feel is achievable will be down to one of these underlying reasons:

1   **They lack confidence in their own ability.** In this instance you need to try to convince them that you think they can do the job. You should challenge their reasons for not believing in their ability. Ask them what support they need, whether from you or from elsewhere, then promise and provide that support. You should 'sell' them the benefits of achieving this goal – it will help them grow as an individual, and further their chances of promotion, higher wages or bonuses. But never tell them to get on with it and see you if they have a problem, because this is telling them that you don't expect to see them unless they fail.

2 **They don't like to be challenged.** They are happy working on something less challenging and want to continue having an easy time. (They aren't going to explain it this way of course – they will probably try to dress it up as number 1, and you will have to use your judgement to spot the truth.) You need to challenge their reasoning. Sometimes the best way is to state a blunt and open case, and encourage a response: "I get the impression that you don't want to take on this objective because you think it sounds too much like hard work. How right am I?" It is putting words into people's mouths but it gets a discussion going. Identify what they think are the obstacles to their achievement of this goal, then either offer them support to overcome each obstacle, or set the overcoming of each obstacle as a subsidiary goal to be achieved first. In the face of uncompromising obstinacy, you may have to fall back on 'selling' them the consequences of refusal to take on these challenging objectives. For example, their job will become increasingly tedious; they will be surpassed for promotion, they will not be in line for a bonus or pay rise; or will be first in line for redundancy.

3 **They fear they are being set up to fail.** Again, follow the strategy outlined in 1. But perhaps you need to be asking yourself some searching questions about your management style if the person literally seems to think that you are setting them up to fail.

Help your people see and agree that goals are genuinely achievable.

3.7

SMART is relevant

You sometimes see a Formula 1 racing driver deliberately lose a race. Why? Well, it might be because his aim is to keep his teammate in the number one position for the Championship. For the rest of us, in the real world, this serves as a reminder that we must keep checking that our people are always working towards the goals of the team or organization.

This may seem blatantly obvious, but I'd be willing to bet that most readers of this book have, at some time in their working lives, asked themselves why they are doing a particular task!

The best way to clarify the relevance of a task is to ask *how* it contributes to all the following:

Aims of the organization	Present quarter	Present financial year	Future
Aims of the department	Present quarter	Present financial year	Future
Aims of the team	Present month	Present quarter	Future
Aims of the individual	Present appraisal cycle	Current role or next role	Career

one minute wonder Take a moment to look at what each of your people is doing at this moment. Is everyone's task relevant to the team's objective? If you cannot genuinely answer yes, you are failing.

Note that the question is *how*. If a task cannot be explained as contributing to any of the current or future aims listed in the table then it is almost certainly not relevant.

■ **Scenario 1.** Let's say you have a Personal Assistant whose role is to assist you. You want to ask that person to collect your dry cleaning from the shop. *How* will that contribute to the various aims? The answer is that it will contribute to your PA's current role and free you up to do more managerial tasks.

■ **Scenario 2.** One of your team members is an architect. You want to ask that person to design an extension for your house during the quiet periods on your work project. *How* will that contribute to the areas on the table? The answer is that it won't, and you shouldn't ask. (Though you can, of course, offer the job as a private commission.)

■ **Scenario 3.** Another of your team members is a computer programmer. You want to ask that person to check the hard drive on your computer and get rid of suspected viruses. *How* will that contribute to the various areas on the table? The answer here is more tricky and depends on the specified role of the programmer. If the job role includes IT support for the team or department, then it's relevant. However, if your organization has separate IT support personnel – it might even be a contract with external specialists – then it would be much better for that third party to check your computer rather than taking up your programmer's time with a task that's possibly outside their area of expertise.

Ensure that all the tasks and goals you set are genuinely relevant.

3.8

SMART is time-bound

Ask anyone in work what wastes their time, and an answer on the lines of "waiting for other people to do their bit so I can get on with mine" usually comes high on the list. Every task needs a time limit or completion date. Even tasks that are not a priority now will become more urgent as time passes.

Have you seen the film *The Bucket List*? It concerns two men in hospital who both discover that they have a short time to live. They make a list of the things they have always wanted to do before they die. The film then follows their activities as they complete all the tasks they want to before the literal 'deadline'. The moral of the story is that, if you don't set a deadline, then things just don't get done.

At work it is important to have appropriate time constraints to tasks. This means several things to you as a manager:

one minute wonder Don't be the kind of manager who is constantly asking for things to be done to unrealistic deadlines. An honest appraisal of the three areas mentioned here will give you a good idea of the genuine time to allow for each individual task.

1 **Work out when the task needs to be completed.** This might involve looking at how the task fits in with other tasks in a schedule. If you've been given a deadline by someone else – perhaps your own boss, another department or a client – check to see if it is a genuine final deadline. It's best if you can see how much leeway there is in all parts of a schedule.

2 **Work out how long the task will take.** You need a reasonable idea of how long the task is going to take the person in question. Remember that different people may fulfil the same task in different timescales according to their level of skill.

3 **Work out how the task fits around the rest of the workload.** You need to know the current workloads of your people when you are planning to delegate tasks. (This is where giving SMART objectives for all tasks makes the overall workloads of different people easier to calculate.) You might need to shuffle tasks among different people or extend other deadlines to accommodate the task.

When you give someone a SMART objective, ideally build in some leeway, working backwards from the final deadline. For example, it's Monday morning now and you find out that a report is needed for a meeting on Thursday; so you tell your team member that their deadline for compiling the report is Wednesday. You also tell them that you will extend the deadline for their other tasks until Friday in order to accommodate the extra work in compiling the report.

Being able to balance the workload with your people's available time is a measure of success for you.

3.9

Know the SHABBY and PRISM approaches

While the SMART approach to goal-setting (Secrets 3.3 to 3.8) works in many situations, you can also try the SHABBY and PRISM approaches.

SHABBY goal setting

When you are writing up a detailed vision of a goal, make sure the SHABBY categories are fulfilled:

■ **S = Subject.** The subject of the goal needs to be clear.
■ **H = Headline.** In the best tradition of journalism, the headline 'tells the story' (explains the goal) in a single, short sentence.
■ **A = Actions.** The actions are the detailed practical steps the participants will put in place to ensure they reach the goal.
■ **BB = Business Benefits.** The business benefits provide the rationale for doing something. There is a view that any objective that doesn't have definite business benefits should be discarded or at least delayed until all other priorities have been completed.
■ **Y = Yes?** This is both a reality check and a commitment to carry out the goal.

> "Once you have given people an objective they understand and can believe in wholeheartedly, then 99% of the time you can leave them to achieve it"

Brigadier Nigel Haynes, 10th PMO Ghurkha Rifles

PRISM goal setting

The PRISM model actually incorporates all points of the SMART process and adds two more.

■ **P = Personal.** This means personal accountability as well as unique.
■ **R = Realistic.** This is similar to the 'Achievable' of SMART and also includes the 'Time-based' element of SMART.
■ **I = Interesting.** People put more effort into something that is of interest to them. Interest could be generated by the personal preference of the individual, the benefit to them in their career or the business benefit of the task.
■ **S = Specific.** The detail of the required outcome, as in SMART.
■ **M = Measurable.** Again, the measurability factor, as in SMART.

Whichever approach you take, you must think really hard about the goals you set your team and individuals.

3.10

Make the mundane more exciting

It is usually easy to set great goals for people in dynamic jobs, such as sales or software development. Most managers find it harder to set motivating goals for people in relatively mundane, if vital, jobs – e.g. cleaners, administrators, shelf stackers. This often leads to the people in such jobs feeling bored or trapped.

Everyone needs a decent goal or objective. People working in jobs perceived as lowly may be keen to prove their worth and progress, while others may be happy to continue with a mundane job but still benefit from some motivation. No one knows a job better than the person doing it, so don't waste time as a manager trying to think up complex individual goals for people in repetitive jobs. Try these approaches:

■ **Set a challenge.** For instance: "Think of ways in which you could do your job in two hours less each week. I'd like you to explain these ways to me in a week from now. If we think this will work, I can… Give you two hours' extra paid leave each week…Teach you how to [something that will benefit the individual]… Let you [do something that is of benefit to the individual]… in the saved time."

"In every job that's to be done there is an element of fun"

Mary Poppins

■ **Set little competitions.** If you have two or more people or teams all doing similar jobs you can get them to compete with each other for a token prize. (Keep the prize at a token level to avoid the competition becoming destructive.) If you have only one person doing a job, you can still set them a competition against their previous performance: to do the job quicker than last week, produce more than last week. In this case, you could offer time off as the prize because the individual will have completed their job by the end.

■ **Try a roundabout approach.** Ask an individual what they would change about their job if they were you. If they suggest changes that can be made with little expenditure, suggest that they try this and see if it helps. If they say that they would change nothing, challenge them: "So you are totally happy with everything about your job? No problems at all? You have all the equipment, materials, time, skills and support that you could ever want?" If they still claim that they would change nothing, set them some time to think about this matter. They are bound to come up with something, even if it is just: "I could use a new mop because the old one is worn out". You can then set them a goal of sourcing the new equipment to their satisfaction for a minimal cost.

Repetitive jobs become all the more boring if there is nothing to aim for.

Motivate yourself and your people

People who are motivated are generally more productive and need less supervision than those who are not. People are motivated by different things, which makes your job as a manager of people more challenging and interesting. This chapter exposes the myth that people are mostly motivated by money and shows how non-financial benefits can help keep your people enthusiastic and happy to work for you.

4.1

Know the hierarchy of needs

People in different situations are motivated by different needs, according to psychologist Abraham Maslow. His work is often referred to as 'Maslow's Pyramid', and it looks like this:

'Self Actualization' Needs
Doing things simply because you want to

'Esteem' Needs
Status, responsibility, a place in the hierarchy

Social Needs
Friendship, support, love

'Keeping' Needs
Safety, security, order (keeping the basics)

Basic Survival Needs
Food, water, shelter, warmth

one minute wonder It is well worth taking a few moments to look at Maslow's Pyramid and ask yourself a few questions: Where am I in terms of my job on Maslow's Pyramid? Where do I think each member of my team is? Where do they think they are? Where does my boss think I am?

That's the theory but what does it mean to a manager?

■ What it means is that, if you have a person who can barely afford to house and feed their family (struggling to meet 'Basic Survival Needs'), then they are unlikely to be motivated by a role/task/job title that carries mainly status (i.e. which appeals to the 'Esteem Needs' aspects).

■ Equally, if you have someone who comes from a wealthy and respected family, they are unlikely to be motivated by a job that pays a low income and has no prospects for the future.

Of course, in the first situation, if the role/task/job title is going to lead quickly to a financial benefit, then a person may be motivated. In the second situation, if the lowly job is purely to learn the basics before taking on responsibility and status, then it may be acceptable.

Many managers face a problem in the 'Social Needs' area. Some staff may welcome the sense of belonging to the company 'club' – they socialize together outside work and value the camaraderie of colleagues. Other staff may have strong social, cultural, religious or family ties and have little or no interest in socializing with work colleagues.

Knowledge is the key to unlocking motivation, and motivation is the key to unlocking high performance.

4.2

Motivate beyond money

A study by Kovach (George Mason University, USA) compared staff members' ranking of what they wanted from their jobs with what their bosses thought was important to the staff. The results showed a great disparity in perceptions!

Ranked order of importance	Managers' opinion	Staff answers
1	Good wages	Interesting work
2	Job security	Appreciation (being appreciated personally and for my work)
3	Promotion	Engagement (kept informed, asked my opinion, empowered)
4	Good working conditions	Job security
5	Interesting work	Good wages

According to this study, managers sometimes disregard the most important motivational techniques when dealing with their staff. We often think monetary incentives are the best way to motivate people, but more often than not non-monetary incentives are best.

Two key managerial points emerged from Kovach's work. The first point is that what most staff want from their jobs can easily be addressed by their immediate team leaders and supervisors, and are relatively inexpensive to implement. The second point is that a person's career position will affect their motivation. For instance, 'interesting work' to a young person might be something technically new or challenging. To someone in mid-career it might be responsibility for others, such as a small team. For someone with a much longer experience, training new starters might be interesting.

Managers should ask themselves the following questions when attempting to provide a better motivational climate for their staff:

■ How often do I personally thank people for a job well done?
■ Do I give feedback in a timely and specific way?
■ Do I meet with and listen to my people on a frequent basis?
■ Have I created an open, trusting and fun workplace?
■ How do I encourage and reward initiative and new ideas?
■ Do I frequently share information about the organization with people?
■ Do I involve people in decisions, especially those that affect them?
■ Do my people feel a sense of ownership of their jobs and the team as a whole?
■ Do I give people enough chances to succeed?
■ Do I reward and recognize people based on their performance?

When you can genuinely answer positively to each and every one of these questions, you will have a well-motivated team.

Motivation is seldom purely financial; it is about the way you manage!

4.3

Identify people's personal motivators

Secrets 4.1 and 4.2 showed that not all people are motivated by the same things. Secret 4.2 clearly showed that it is easy and quite common for managers to misdiagnose the motivators of their staff. The only real safe way to identify what motivates a person is to have a discussion with them.

As a manager or leader you need to ensure that you balance all your decisions to reflect the needs of the Task, the Team and the Individual – this is the Action Centred Leadership of Secret 1.3. The very act of discussing motivation with your people shows them that you do consider them to be individuals, and that you value them and want to engage them. Here is a straightforward way to initiate, carry out and follow through such a discussion:

■ **Initiation.** You need to get to know your team members as individuals, so you need to have one-to-one discussions with each of them as a general part of your role. You can do this formally, by booking a suitable time and place and letting the person know in advance that you want to talk with them. Alternatively you might choose to have these discussions on a less formal basis, by simply going to the person's workstation, catching them by the drinks machine or – if you are both smokers – going and having a discussion over a cigarette.

■ **Carrying out a discussion.** It is probably not productive to ask, "What motivates you?", as this sounds a little mechanistic. Start off getting to know something of the person's private life. Do they have a spouse, children or dependent parents? What do they do in their spare time? Ask what makes them happy. Ask them to describe a perfect day or week at work. What makes a perfect weekend or day off? Does this happen often? If not, why not? Ask what they want to get from the organization over the next 12 months and what they see as their current career goal. Listen to their answers, and try to make the conversation flow rather than being an interrogation. Be prepared to share your personal information with them – this isn't weakness or over familiarity but an expression of trust, partnership and belonging to the same team.

■ **Following up.** You should make some confidential notes, because you can't expect to remember everything for all your team members, especially if there are more than three or four of them. You will be able to identify rewards to offer people and to tailor your appreciation according to individual preferences. You will be able to decide who best to allocate or delegate tasks to in relation to people's references and aspirations. In short, you can help people to motivate themselves!

When you know what motivates a person, you can give them things that encourage self-motivation... Result!

4.4

Influence people to want what you want

If you can use *influence* to encourage people to want the same end result as you, then you won't have to work so hard to *coerce* them. 'Work so hard' in this instance means supervise, micro-manage and check.

You must recognize that different people and situations call for different approaches. On some occasions you can use a purely logical argument: "Buy this one: it is cheaper." On some occasions you have to use an ethical argument: "Buy this one: it is the brand that your mother, who you love and trust, always uses." On other occasions you have to use an empathetic argument: "Buy this one: it is the one you have had before so you'll feel safe."

■ **Logical approach.** The logical approach is based solely on empirical data. In theory, you'd think that this would always be adequate to influence someone to do something.

■ **Ethical approach.** Humans aren't entirely logical, however. We are influenced by what other people are doing or thinking. The more we respect a person and feel we share their values, the more likely we are to emulate them. Similarly, the less we respect the person, the less likely we are to emulate them. In this instance we don't need to be referring to someone we know personally. The fact that footballer David Beckham endorses a product influences people's buying decisions. The fact that the 'Surgeon General' puts a heath warning on cigarettes influences people's decision to smoke or not. Some will stop because the 'Surgeon General' is a medical name they trust. Conversely, some will smoke because they don't like being told what to do by the government!

■ **Empathetic approach.** Finally we come to the empathetic argument – appealing to how a course of action will make a person feel. Unless you know a person quite well, you can only make an informed guess as to how something will make them feel, and – as we saw in Secret 4.2 – we can get it spectacularly wrong. This should make it clear that, as a leader or manager, you really do need to get to know your people. The traditional idea of a leader being aloof from the people he or she leads is definitely a dying concept.

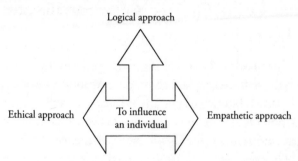

You need to find the right mix of logical, ethical and empathetic argument to influence each individual to want to do what you want them to do. If you can find this balance, you will be a good manager of people; if you don't, you will find that your life becomes much harder and your people will not follow you unless forced.

Leadership is a relationship that you have to work at.

4.5

'Catch' people doing things right

Most people hold the opinion that bosses only ever appear to catch them doing something wrong. "If I haven't heard from or seen the boss, then everything must be OK." "Oh, no, here comes the boss. What have I done wrong this time?"

They hold this opinion for a reason: historically the boss only spoke to the staff to complain about poor performance or to tell people to work harder. But it is important to break the cycle of the bad-news-boss. In order to do this, you have first to be seen around your people, regularly and frequently. This is called 'management by wandering about'! Then you have to get people used to you 'catching' them doing things right. You don't have to make a big deal over it – just a few brief words of appreciation or thanks for a job well done, a tidy work area,

one minute wonder Take at least one minute every day to practise 'management by wandering about' and deliberately trying to 'catch' people doing things right. You'll be amazed how quickly people start to look forward to seeing you.

presentable customer-facing staff, a good window display, etc. The following phrases might help:

- I'm impressed by…
- Well done on…
- …is a good piece of work
- Thank you for…
- That's nice…
- That's excellent…
- I'm happy to see…
- My boss is pleased to hear that…
- I'm pleased to see...
- Congratulations on…
- That's good…
- Perfect…
- You're doing well…
- Show me how that works…
- I like that…

Don't save these things up until later: say them when you see the person, even if you are complimenting a member of staff in front of a customer. Indeed, this raises the person's stock with the customer, and tells the customer that the organization values its staff. If the people you are complimenting are part of a sub-team, make sure you also compliment the team leader: "Well done, Jo, your team does you proud!"

Be sure that you don't just compliment people you know or like. Compliment everyone who has done something worthy of a compliment, even if the only thing you can compliment them on is actually arriving at work on time. But…*never* issue a compliment immediately followed by a complaint, because it devalues the compliment. For example,"I'm pleased to see the team all here on time today. Let's see if we can avoid the mistakes you made yesterday."

People who feel appreciated are motivated. Remember Secret 4.2? Being appreciated was the second most important motivator to staff!

When you 'catch' people doing things right, they look forward to seeing you and become your willing followers.

4.6

Empower your people

You empower people when you let them take a level of authority themselves. Empowerment is counter-intuitive to many managers who might think: "I have been selected, trained, entrusted and paid as a manager; is it right that I should empower my staff to do what I ought to be responsible for?"

What empowerment really is

■ Giving people more responsibility for their own jobs and actions.
■ Asking people for their opinions and then considering their answers.
■ Explaining the reasons why things are done, but letting people select the best way to do them.
■ Letting people succeed.
■ Letting people learn from their mistakes.
■ Encouraging people to use their intelligence, rather than expecting them to act like machines.
■ Allowing people to reach their full potential.
■ Nurturing people's strengths and helping them overcome weaknesses.
■ Giving people the right to choose their behaviour and the responsibility to accept the consequences.
■ Being strong and confident enough to accept that you cannot control everything personally.

What empowerment is not

■ Allowing a situation of anarchy to develop.
■ Leaving the team to fight it out amongst themselves, with survival of the fittest.
■ Washing your hands of responsibility for anything going wrong.
■ Allowing people to make massive mistakes that will be irretrievable.
■ Sitting back and watching a seriously dangerous situation develop.
■ Accepting the perks of a manager's job title but not the responsibility that goes with it.

If you recall Secret 4.2, the top five motivators for staff were: 1. Interesting work; 2. Appreciation; 3. Engagement; 4. Job security; 5. Good wages.

Empowering people – offering them more responsibility – fulfils the top three of those motivators:

■ **1. Interesting work.** People will find their job more interesting if they have more responsibility for their own work.
■ **2. Appreciation.** Empowerment proves to a person that you appreciate them because you are placing trust in them and showing that you think they are competent and capable.
■ **3. Engagement.** Empowerment enables a person to engage with their work, their colleagues and you more than when they are simply told what to do.

You may be reluctant to empower someone you barely know, but try to give everyone a degree of authority as soon as possible.

4.7

Practise the art of delegating

Delegating tasks to your people is a major part of empowering and motivating them. Like empowerment, though, delegation can feel counter-intuitive, especially to a person new to management. You need to practise the art of delegating.

In Secret 1.5 you learned how to delegate a task successfully using the STAR approach: that is, ensuring that the person has the Skills, Tools, Authority and Responsibility to do the job.

Delegation will have numerous benefits, not only for you (giving you more time to manage) but also for your people. By delegating tasks you test the ability and potential of your people. Their jobs will be more varied, interesting and fulfilling, they will have a chance to prove their worth to you, and they will learn and grow as employees.

When you are delegating always remember the following things.

1 Ensure you give the employee a 'STAR', as it were, for every task you delegate (see Secret 1.5 for more details).

"If you can't get a day's work done in a working day, you aren't delegating enough"

AJS Edington, British army officer and mountaineer

2 Don't delegate only to the people you've already tried and decided to trust. If you do this, those people will begin to resent your constant imposition, and they will also be resented by others who will see them as your favourites.

3 Don't delegate just the jobs you personally dislike or are bad at, or just the jobs that are lousy. This will be seen as laziness.

4 Conversely, delegate some of the jobs you enjoy and that other people are likely to enjoy. This will be seen as a gift.

5 If you have a person who thinks they can do your job better than you, delegating jobs to them is a good way to prove to them that life as a manager isn't as easy as they might think!

6 Delegate jobs to test people and help them build up their skills and experience before you promote them.

7 Delegate jobs to give yourself time to supervise, manage, coach and support your people.

You can empower and motivate people with careful delegation.

4.8

Support your people

Your people should always be able to rely on you to support them. 'Support', however, doesn't always mean the same thing. You must adapt your approach to different individuals and situations.

■ **Scenario 1.** If someone has made a dreadful mistake they may think that your 'support' will be in covering up for them. In reality it may be best for them to face up to their error. Support might mean representing them to authority, giving them a character witness and helping them to see ways of putting right their mistake.

■ **Scenario 2.** If someone declares a desire for promotion and you do not believe that they have the capacity to succeed, would it be in their best interests for you to recommend them? No! It would be setting

> **case study** Think of the analogy of a parent with a child learning to ride a bike. At first 'support' means holding the bike upright whilst the child gets used to the pedals and handlebars, and the need to balance. Then 'support' means going at a walking pace. A few goes later, 'support' means a lighter hand holding the bike upright as you run along behind and the child

them up for failure. Support in this instance might mean helping them to see why you lack faith in them at this stage of their career, what they need to do to consolidate their position and develop themselves to a situation where you can wholeheartedly support their application.

■ Scenario 3. If a person has a seriously inflated opinion of his or her own ability, support might mean allowing them to fail! By giving this person the responsibility of the role without making it a substantive promotion, you let them discover for themselves that they are not yet ready for the full weight of the permanent position.

■ Scenario 4. If someone is lacking in confidence and continually comes to you for your advice and backing, by always giving it you may be reinforcing 'learned dependency'. The person will never gain the confidence in their own convictions and will permanently need your approval, sanction, consent or permission. Support in this instance will mean forcing the person to make their own decisions. This could be through delegation (see Secrets 1.5 and 4.7) or simply by explaining to the person how capable they really are.

Supporting your people is your job; how best to support them is a judgement that you have to make.

pedals faster, gaining their own equilibrium. After another few goes, 'support' means persuading the child that he or she can ride when you let go. Then 'support' may mean persuading a child with skinned knees and a shaken confidence to get back on the bike. Finally, 'support' means letting the child out on their bike without any supervision.

Manage good performance

You might be tempted to leave the good performers to get on with their job without intervention, and to a great extent you can. However, you have a vital management role to play with people who produce good results – you must recognize and reward their success; you must maintain and nurture it; you must encourage people to learn from their success; and you must ensure that you keep these people in an environment where they can flourish.

5.1

Identify good performance

The most obvious example of good performance is the successful achievement of the goals that you agreed with the individual. But does that automatically mean that someone failing to achieve a goal has performed badly? What about someone who achieves something that wasn't actually set as a goal?

People's performance isn't always something that can be quantified and added up on a spreadsheet. If it were, managers would be unnecessary and could be replaced by a simple desktop computer! Performance needs to be managed with judgement and human thought, and this goes for success as well as poor performance.

Here are examples of good performance.

1 **Targets hit and goals achieved.** If an individual hits their targets and achieves all their goals, then they have returned good performance and should be commended and rewarded. Be aware that people have been known to manipulate figures to hit targets (check the scenario in point 2 of Secret 6.1). Also be clear in your mind about the value of the target itself – was it set at an appropriate level? Some managers get into the mindset of automatically assuming that if someone has achieved their targets it must mean that their targets were too low!

2 **Acceptable levels of activity and effort.** A goal may have been missed through sheer bad luck or factors entirely outside the control or influence of the individual. The person may have approached the task with consideration and made a supreme effort, despite failing to achieve the target.

3 **'Going the extra mile.'** Medals are awarded in the military for conduct above and beyond the call of duty. Similarly, you should identify effort, achievement or output that is over the expected norm in your workplace.

4 **Self-motivated improvement.** When a member of your team uses their initiative to provide a better or different service, or to improve something for themselves or their team, they deserve to be recognized for good performance.

5 **Teamworking.** When a team member has fulfilled his or her goals (or at least done everything they can to fulfil them) and then goes to the aid of a colleague, say, this is worthy enough to be recognized as good performance.

Don't think only in terms of goals and targets – look also at effort, initiative and teamwork.

5.2

Reward good performance

A reward might mean a pay rise or other financial bonus, but don't worry if you are not actually in a position to offer this to your good performers. Secrets 4.2 and 4.3 covered non-financial motivators – you can use these as rewards, too.

Here are four real-life examples of rewards to staff.

■ **Example 1.** A fit and active but unqualified school leaver proved himself to be an asset to the team. He achieved his personal goals, helped others, suggested improvement ideas and generally set a great example to his peers. His boss wanted to reward this man and used all his influence to get the young man accepted into the organization's graduate training programme, despite the fact that the youngster had left school early, without qualifications. Five years later the young man was running a division of the organization.

■ **Example 2.** A customer wanted a service that required a couple of people to work through a weekend at short notice. The manager asked head office for authorization for overtime plus an extra day of holiday for the people who provided the service. She asked her team for volun-

one minute wonder Keep handy a supply of inexpensive small rewards – desk toys, chocolates, doughnuts, etc – and make an effort to reward little acts of success and effort.

teers, telling them they would get overtime rates, but not mentioning the extra day off. She got two people, who delivered an excellent service for the customer. On the Sunday night the manager rewarded the two workers by offering the unexpected day off, to be taken when they wanted. (This is called Planned Spontaneous Recognition – although you planned it, it looks spontaneous!)

■ **Example 3.** A small group produced a report and submitted it to the boss. The following day the boss invited the report team into his office because he had something he wanted to say to them. The group gathered, apprehensive that they had done something wrong. But the boss opened his briefcase and got out a box of doughnuts, which he passed round whilst asking who had done what and who had thought up which great idea in the really impressive report. The box of doughnuts cost a few cents; the effect was worth hundred of dollars.

■ **Example 4.** A hard-working army mechanic was lying under a digger repairing the hydraulics when someone tapped his foot and asked if he wanted a coffee. He replied, "Yes mate, white, two sugars." Five minutes later his foot was tapped again, "Coffee's ready". He slid out from under the tractor to be handed a steaming mug… by the Major General. The gesture cost the army nothing.

A personal human gesture can be the most valuable reward.

5.3

Help people learn from good performance

We tend to talk about learning from mistakes, but we should also encourage people to learn from their successes as well. Mistakes mainly tell us how *not* to do something – we ideally need to learn from something that works. Your people's good performance works!

This secret gives a six-step process to help people learn from good performance. It is a process in which most of your role is being the guardian of the question, rather than the provider of the answers.

By going through a process like this frequently, your people will learn 'intentionally' from each success rather than simply hoping that they will get into a habit after several successes. It also allows you to develop a guideline for 'Best Practice' to be passed on to others.

"The greatest compliment that was ever paid me was when one asked me what I thought, and attended to my answer" Henry David Thoreau, 19th-century American writer

Step	Purpose	Benefit
1. Identify and describe briefly your person's successful performance.	To ensure public recognition / mutual understanding of the good performance.	Person will be pleased, self-aware, and everyone will acknowledge the success.
2. Ask how it went. You might have to prompt here: "I thought that was excellent. What do you think?"	Opportunity to give further praise, engage with person, encourage self-appraisal.	The person starts to appraise and judge their own performance.
3. Ask what parts went well. Also ask why they went well.	To encourage a more detailed analysis of the task from the person who did the work.	The person will personally assess how hard / easy / complex / simple / challenging the task was.
4. Summarize the reasons for the success.	Again, public recognition / mutual understanding of the good performance, this time in more detail.	The person hears you further praising their work. Other people might also hear the praise.
5. Ask them what they would do differently next time.	To pick up little things that could be done better.	The person knows what they skimped on or had to go back and do again – it is more self-appraisal.
6. Ask, "What have you learned from this?"	To summarize 'Best Practice' of things to repeat and things to change.	Revises in person's mind what works and what can be done to improve.

It is faster to learn from success than failure. It is also cheaper and less embarrassing.

5.4

Maintain good performance in a crisis

It's all very well to focus on good performance when things are going well. However, it's all too easy to lose focus when times are hard, when you're facing a crisis and possibly your job itself is threatened. When the going gets tough, the tough get going!

The day-to-day management of your people is usually the first thing to be sidelined when things get hard. What tends to happen is that managers lock themselves away and pore over spreadsheets, looking for cost-cutting initiatives and targeting anything that won't be producing an instant profit this quarter. In the words of Tom Peters in his leader-

case study This case study is included in Tom Peters' training video, 'The Leadership Alliance', mentioned above. A General Motors factory in Bay City, Michigan, was under notice of closure. Labour relations were poor, productivity low, wastage and scrap high. The video shows a new manager, Pat Carrigan, taking over the plant. Her first move was to walk around the plant speaking to workers, asking their opinions and listen-

ship training video, *The Leadership Alliance:* "You start a paper-clip counting campaign and start calculating how many bodies you have to lay-off." Sadly these things are usually counter-productive in the medium and long term.

Interesting challenges, appreciation and engagement were the top three staff motivators identified in Secret 4.2, and you can and must still provide these things when times are tough. Especially since the next two items on the list – job security and good wages – are under threat.

Unless you own the company you cannot give any guarantees about job security or wages – you may even be having to impose selective lay-offs and/or pay freezes/cuts. This makes the provision of the interest, appreciation and engagement even more important.

Even when you and your organization are not in a major crisis, there is probably constant pressure of targets and changing environments. In these circumstances it is all too easy to forget about encouraging good performance, celebrating successes and recognizing effort. However, strong leadership and support on your part will help keep your people positive through difficult times, even in situations when redundancy is inevitable (see case study below).

The real test of your leadership is when things are tough – it is also when your leadership is most important.

ing to their answers. She had the place repainted and continued the social and community activities of the plant. She did not use her office. At first, people were suspicious of her, but Pat continued to appreciate and engage with shop floor workers every day. Productivity rose, absenteeism dropped, scrappage and waste dropped. This good performance continued up until the day the plant finally had to close.

5.5

Beware the 'Peter Principle'

Why do many organizations seem to be full of people who aren't capable of doing the job they are paid to do? Why are so many IT project managers unable to manage a project? Why are so many call centre team leaders clueless about how to lead a team? It is usually a result of the 'Peter Principle' in action.

Dr. Laurence J. Peter and Raymond Hull first espoused what has become known as the 'Peter Principle' in their 1968 book of the same name. The premise is this: people are promoted based upon their performance in a job, but the job they are promoted to is not the job for which their performance was assessed. The authors described such people as having been 'promoted to their level of incompetence'.

For example, the excellent analyst programmer is rewarded for good performance by being promoted to the role of project manager. As project manager, this person no longer does what he or she is good at – analysing and programming – and is not very happy in the new role. You now have someone with little skill in the requirements of their new job and little will to do it. If the environment (in this instance the company culture) accepts poor performance, then the individual will simply be allowed to continue inefficiently. If the culture doesn't tolerate poor performance, then the individual will probably become a slave driver, forcing his or her team to fill in and cover up for their manager's ineptitude.

People seldom turn down a promotion, and organizations seldom demote managers. This is how the 'Peter Principle' happens.

Ways to avoid the 'Peter Principle'

■ Try to reward people without building expectations that rewards should necessarily mean rising up the hierarchy.

■ Make all promotions dependent on a probationary period.

■ Have someone act as unpaid deputy manager for a period before being ratified with a substantive promotion.

■ If possible, create a technical advancement scale, separating it from the management scale. This will enable you to give people kudos and extra pay for specialist or technical roles rather than just for management responsibility.

■ Ascertain what an individual's career aspirations are before offering a promotion. (A promotion is a gift; it is churlish to refuse!)

■ Insist that people are trained for the new role *before* they are considered for promotion.

If you have to manage someone who has already reached their level of incompetence, try to find ways to move them back to their level of competence. A sideways move to technical consultancy, for example, might allow the aforementioned analyst programmer to train others in what he or she is really good at, without having to manage a project.

Promoting someone to their level of incompetence benefits no one – not the person, not their staff, not the customers and certainly not you!

Manage poor performance

Probably the single most diffi-cult thing for many managers is dealing with poor performance. Some managers just put up with the problem. However, if you tolerate poor performance, the people who are performing poorly continue in the same way, and the people who were performing well wonder why they bother. The poor performers will stay with you because you make their life easy, while the good performers will quit. Ultimately you will be deemed a failure!

6.1

Identify poor performance

In order to identify poor performance, you have to know what acceptable performance should look like. There are two elements to identifying this: the actual outcome of the person's performance and the way that outcome was achieved.

Failure to achieve a goal

In Chapter 3 you learned to make plans and set meaningful goals. So long as a goal was fair in the first place (see SMART goal-setting in Secret 3.3), then failure to achieve that goal is a case of poor performance. For example, you have a team of sales reps and each agrees to the goal to sell 200 cans of soft drink at a minimum price of 25 cents a can by the end the month. One team member has sold only 120 cans, all at the minimum price, and cannot offer a reasonable excuse. It's a clear case of poor performance.

Failure in the way the goal was achieved

Performance isn't just about getting the goal achieved though; there may also be concerns about the way in which a goal is achieved. For example, by the 25th of the month another team member has sold all 200 cans to one customer at a price of 35 cents a can. They have achieved their goal. Success! However, the customer has lodged a complaint: they were under the impression that they were ordering 440ml cans, but when the delivery took place the cans turned out to be 225ml. Your team member either deliberately misled the customer in order to make the target, or generally wasn't clear enough about the product. This is not only an example of poor performance, it will also have a detrimental effect on your team in the future.

Failure to avoid failure

With the same goal as above, another team member reaches the end of the month having sold only 30 cans, all of which were in the first week of the month. The individual visited lots of potential customers in the last three weeks but was not able to make any sales. The person's excuse for this is that the largest competitor in their region started to sell an identical product for 15 cents a can on the third of the month.

In this instance is there a case of poor performance and if so, what is it?

The poor performance here may be that the individual failed to inform you as soon as they were aware of the change in the market situation that affected their ability to achieve their goal. If they had done so, you might have been able to renegotiate their goal to one that was achievable. For example, you could have changed the negotiating terms to match the competitor's price in that region, or decided not to match the competitor's price but instead redistribute the workload across team members in different regions.

You need unequivocal evidence of poor performance before you can confront it.

6.2

Confront an instance of poor performance

Once you have objective evidence that a task has been performed poorly, you need to confront it. Many managers find this a very hard thing to do. You should remind yourself that you are *confronting poor performance*, not *starting a confrontation* with a team member, and follow the guidelines here.

There are seven areas to consider when confronting an instance of poor performance, which will make it an altogether easier activity to get right. Following these rules take the chance out of the matter, and you will notice that the points of consideration spell the word **LOTTERY**.

1 **L = Location.** It is usually counter-productive to criticize someone in front of their colleagues or customers, so you will want to deal with the matter out of earshot of any listeners. This could be in a relatively informal setting – by the water cooler, in the lift or while walking across the car park. For more serious instances of poor performance, you could make it more formal by arranging a meeting in a private room.

2 **O = Objective.** This sounds odd but you need to decide exactly what you want to achieve by confronting the poor performance. For example, you might want simply to tell the person that their performance was noticed and wasn't acceptable; to find out why they did something; to give them a solution to their poor performance; or you might want to encourage them to solve their problem themselves.

3 **T = Timing.** You need to address an instance of poor performance as soon as possible after the failure has taken place.

4 **T = Target.** You are confronting the instance of poor performance, not the actual person. "The task was done too slowly"; not, "You are too slow."

5 **E = Emotions.** If you feel angry and upset before you start, then you will find it harder to be objective. Likewise, if the other person is upset before you start, they may say or do something they later regret.

6 **R = Reactions.** Both yours and theirs – if the discussion starts to get heated or overly emotional, be prepared to stop and reconvene later.

7 **Y = "Yes".** You want to have a positive outcome from this discussion. That outcome is based on your objective, whether it is, "Yes, I was wrong, and it won't happen again", or, "Yes, we have found a solution."

Don't wait for the 'right moment' to come along before confronting poor performance. The 'right moment' never comes by itself.

6.3

Coach a poor performer to improve

The previous Secret showed you how to confront an instance of poor performance, whereas this Secret shows how you can coach a poor performer so that they see for themselves how to improve. Discuss issues with them and question their behaviour in the way described here.

There are many ways to improve a person's performance, but if you can help them to find their own way to improve themselves, this gives added benefits. Firstly, the person takes ownership of the solution, rather than just doing what you tell them to do. Secondly, they begin to learn that they can improve, which means that they will do so without your intervention in the future.

One of the best ways to achieve this is to spend more of your time and energy asking the right questions than aiming to be the provider of answers. It is a form of coaching, rather than teaching, and similar to the approach you should take when helping people to learn from good performance (see Secret 5.3).

Step	Purpose	Benefit
1. Clearly outline the poor performance.	To ensure open communication and clarity.	Shows respect for the person. Tough on behaviour not person.
2. State impact on goals of person and team.	To establish your concern and the consequences of the poor performance.	Focuses on the bigger picture – the results and outcomes of the failure.
3. Ask person for their point of view. Make sure you genuinely listen and react to the answer!	To get the whole picture, all the evidence.	Encourages open communication, shows your respect for them, engages them.
4. Ask the person what they can do to improve their performance.	To encourage person to take ownership of the problem and find a solution that they think is within their ability.	Person does the work, makes your life easier. Shows respect and confidence from you.
5. Ask what help they need from you and others. Again, genuinely listen and respond to what they say.	To ensure they have the resources and ability to succeed.	Shows appreciation. Increases likelihood of success. Is positive and supportive.
6. Ask the person to summarize the plan that arises from 4 and 5 above, including their proposals for review.	To ensure that both parties are focused on the future and have a mutual understanding of the way forward.	Clarity regarding future action. Emphasizes that the person can control the solution.
7. Ask final 'qualifying' question: "If we do the things outlined in this plan, can you guarantee me that your performance will improve?"	To give a final opportunity to 'reality check' the discussion.	Increases likelihood of success. Increases the person's ownership of the outcome.

Encourage your poor performer to work out how to improve themselves.

6.4

Monitor a poor performer

Some managers assume they have to monitor a poor performer by watching their every move and criticizing their every action. However, that approach is usually counterproductive. You should monitor them in a way that is supportive and includes you 'catching' them doing things right. There are three phases to more supportive monitoring.

Phase 1: gathering evidence

This is the period after your first inkling that a person's performance is going off-track. During this phase you are watching, listening and gathering evidence that the person's behaviour is genuinely awry. By building up this evidence, you give yourself the confidence to confront the poor performance. If poor performance is straightforward failure to achieve a target, then this phase may be exceedingly short – the few minutes it takes between seeing the sales figures, say, and speaking to the person. If the performance failure is something more subtle, such as repeated minor lateness or a slow reduction of output, then this phase will take longer. (But it should never take from now until the person's next annual appraisal!)

Phase 2: reviewing

Once you've had the discussion about improving performance (see previous Secret), there will be a period of monitoring until the performance reaches an acceptable level. This is the period when managers are most likely to adopt a hawk-like critical posture, but you should avoid doing this. Take these actions instead:

■ Check that they are getting any support agreed in step 5 of the coaching steps (see previous Secret).
■ Deliberately aim to 'catch' them doing things right (see Secret 4.5).
■ Refer to and praise progress against the plan they summarized in step 6 of the coaching steps (see previous Secret).
■ Express confidence in their improvement.

At this point you are using the so-called 'Hawthorne Effect' to good benefit – the fact that people's behaviour and output can improve simply when they know they are being watched and measured.

Make sure you have at least one other meeting in which you review the improved performance.

Phase 3: easing-off

This is the easing-off period after the review of improvement has ascertained that the performance is now back up to an acceptable level. During this phase you want to continue 'catching' the person doing things right and appreciating their work, but not overtly. Monitor discreetly to ensure that the Hawthorne effect was not the only thing responsible for the improvement.

Be supportive and positive. Look for evidence of improvements rather than criticizing every fault.

6.5

'Manage out' a very poor performer

If someone performs poorly, your first effort should focus on trying to get him or her back on track. If that doesn't work, you try again. And if that doesn't work…? Ultimately you have to make a decision: is it worth continuing to try to improve the poor performer or would you prefer them off your team?

Options for dealing with a persistent poor performer:

■ **Dismiss the person.** 'Fire' or 'sack' are the common terms for terminating someone's employment. You need to be sure of the employment conditions, however, if you are considering sacking someone. Legal protections in many countries can make it difficult to dismiss employees, even if they are performing badly. If someone is working on contract, however, then you could justify not renewing their contract.

■ **Redeploy the person.** If the person has other skills that are valuable to the organization then it makes sense to move the person into an area where they can utilize those skills. Beware, however, of simply finding a sinecure role for the person (see jargon buster).

■ **'Manage out' the person.** This is the action of coaching the individual to realize for themselves that they are unsuited to this role or task, and so voluntarily decide to move on to another organization without stigma and with your full support. Have another private meeting and ask questions such as: "Is your career advancing while you aren't succeeding?"; "Do you think you might be happier in a job where you can succeed more regularly?"; "What things would you put on a CV to present to another employer?"

There is a little quasi-scientific equation that will help you to decide which course of action to take:

Performance = Skill + Will

What this means is that a person needs to have the ability and skill to do a job, and they need to have the desire and will to do it.

If you know that the person has the skill (perhaps because you have trained them extensively or they used to do the job well) but they still repeatedly fail, then it is clearly the will that is lacking. This is not within your control; it is entirely within theirs. If the person is genuinely keen and enthusiastic but still regularly fails, then it is the skill that is lacking. If they have been trained extensively then it is a skill they simply cannot gain.

Good Skill No Will = Dismiss or 'manage out'.
No Skill Good Will = Redeploy or 'manage out'.
No Skill No Will   = Dismiss or 'manage out'.

Persistent poor performance is infectious. Ideally, 'manage out' the person who has no will to improve.

6.6

Analyse your own performance

All too often, when things go a bit awry, managers start sacking people or blaming people for not following their lead, when they should be striving to improve their own performance. Here is a list of statements about leadership and management for you to ponder.

1 When the people are not following, it's usually the leaders who are lost, not the people. Managers get lost because of isolation, delusion, arrogance, plain stupidity, etc., but above all because they become obsessed with imposing their authority, instead of truly leading.

2 Leading and managing are about helping people achieve a shared vision, not just telling people what to do.

3 Loyalty to a leader relies on the leader having a connection with and understanding of people's needs, wishes and possibilities.

4 Prior to expecting anyone to follow, a manager first needs to demonstrate belief in a vision worthy of following.

5 A leader or manager cannot behave in any way that he or she asks people not to. People have a much keener sense of honesty and integrity than most managers realize.

6 People are a lot cleverer than many managers think. They generally know the answers that elude their managers – they just need the right environment to help their manager to manage.

7 A manager who makes big mistakes should come clean and admit it. People generally forgive mistakes but they do not tolerate managers covering up.

8 A mistake is an opportunity to show remorse and a lesson learned, and then to get better. This goes for your own mistakes and your people's too. Everyone messes up now and then; "to err is human".

9 A good manager should be brave enough to talk when a lesser manager wants to fight. Any fool can resort to threats and aggression. The nature of humankind and civilization is to become more civilized. Leaders should enable not obstruct this process.

Ask yourself, "Am I still worthy of my job?" If the answer is "No", put the problems right!

Periodically reasses your own beliefs and attitudes about leadership and management.

Develop your people

Developing your people is an important part of your role as a leader or manager. The more you train people and give them opportunities to progress, the more benefits you and they will enjoy. Your commitment to development motivates them and shows that you care about them as people. It also shows that you are not afraid of them as potential competitors for your job. This proves your trust, and trust is almost always repaid.

7.1

Commit to developing your people

You might be in an organization that has established systems in place for developing people's skills and experience. If not, you should still give serious thought to what training would benefit your individual team members and the team as a whole. Commit a portion of your time, budget and energy to development, even if this has been neglected in the past.

You and your people should be developing all the time – developing technical knowledge and skills, developing managerial ability or even just keeping up with the changing pace of life.

This all sounds very well, and, indeed, ideas about development often start out seemingly well. The manager has an annual appraisal with an employee and they discuss plans for development over the next 12 months. It's obvious that extra training will help the employee, the team and the manager. However, as the employee reaches the end of the appraisal cycle, he or she realizes that nothing has been done about the training – the manager has been dealing with unexpected problems on the project, etc, and seems to have forgotten what they had discussed.

■ **Make a mental commitment.** You need to make a conscious effort to commit to development, or it will fall by the wayside. If you don't commit, people will assume all sorts of things about you: you don't care about them; you don't keep your word; you only pretended to commit to make it look like you cared; you don't do your job properly; or even that you are scared of developing your people in case they then replace, or worse, surpass you! No matter what happens during the year to distract, deflect, annoy, worry or just occupy you, you must develop your people and also yourself. You also have to make sure that people realize you are developing them.

■ **Create a team development plan.** One way to get started is to write up an outline of ideas about training and development and keep it visible somewhere. It is often the 'keep it visible' bit that is most valuable, otherwise plans are often put into a drawer and never looked at again. If you can post the team development plan on a whiteboard or bulletin board, this keeps it visible for all the team. However, if there are some things on the plan that specific team members don't want publicized, then you should keep it more discreetly in your office or on your PC. One manager I came across actually set it as his screensaver!

■ **Work out some objectives and strategies.** Alongside your goals and objectives relating to the current project or workload, set yourself targets to further the development plan on a weekly or monthly basis. Encourage your staff to take some responsibility for pushing for their own development as well. Plan development activities into the team schedule as you would plan holidays. Schedule a regular team development session once a week, where people can share and discuss what they have learned this week from their jobs. This is a great way to foster the team ethos as well.

Making a genuine commitment to development is the first hurdle.

7.2

Develop people on a tight budget

There are numerous reasons why development plans are abandoned, not least of which is lack of funds. But it is perfectly possible to develop people on a modest budget – even for free.

Very often the problem is that we equate 'development' with 'training', and professional training can cost quite a lot of money. There are the course fees, the staff downtime salary, lost productivity or temp replacement costs, training materials, room hire, subsistence, travel expenses and overnight costs. However, the actual objective is to improve a person's knowledge or skills, and there are many ways to do this that don't involve going on a training course. Some methods have extra benefits as well, as you can see opposite.

"All that is valuable in human society depends upon the opportunity for development accorded the individual" **Albert Einstein**

Development method	Benefits
Learning from another team member who has the knowledge or skill.	Boosts the ego of the skilled person. Ensures the training is relevant. Allows you to test the learner on-site.
Reading a book on the subject.	Learner works at their own pace. Book can be passed on to another team member.
Working through online e-learning modules.	Learners work at their own pace. E-learning is often free or at minimal cost.
Researching a relevant subject and writing a 'paper' on it, which can be presented to the rest of the team, senior managers or even clients.	Learner works at their own pace. Research, writing and presentation are skills in themselves worth learning. The presentation boosts the image of the individual and team.
Running informal sessions ('lunch and learn') in which team members are regarded as subject experts and talk about topics relevant to the team.	Boosts egos of subject experts, spreads learning, allows people to practise designing and delivering a training session.
Swapping jobs. Individual team members swap roles with each other for a period, e.g. a month.	Team members become multi-skilled. Learn to accept and welcome change. People new to a role often see ways to improve processes.
Arranging secondments, attachments or detached duty outside of the team or organization.	Learn best practice from other teams or organizations. Often the most refreshing option for people who have worked for a long time in a certain role. Good for PR.
Offering to help with community projects, e.g. school or college open days, local or national charities, not-for-profit organizations.	Appeals to people's 'Esteem Needs' (Secret 4.1). People learn extra-curricular skills. Good for PR.

Expensive courses are not the only way to develop people's knowledge and skills. Think of other methods.

7.3

Help people leave their 'comfort zones'

People often say, "This is the way things are done here" or "It's the way I do things". The longer someone has been doing something in a certain way, the more likely they will resist the idea of change. Some people resist change of any kind. But we should all make an effort to get out of our 'comfort zone' now and then.

Unfortunately getting out of your comfort zone is… well, uncomfortable! It is a risk: you know what you are good at and you want to stay being good, whereas if you try something else you might not be so good.

We have already looked at some things that get your people out of their comfort zones – job swaps, secondments, detached duty and giving presentations are all activities that may present challenges to people. These challenges will help people to become more accepting of change, or even more enthusiastic about embracing change.

Opposite is another quite radical idea that will help you and your people step out of your comfort zones as well as providing some further development.

one minute wonder Take a moment to look at your 'to do' list and the weekly activities of your people. Deliberately look for tasks that you can swap among people to help them come out of their comfort zones. Reallocate those tasks, and tell people why.

Be inspired by geese

Have you ever noticed that geese fly in a ⋀ shape formation, and that they honk all the time? Each goose gets extra lift from its neighbours, which makes it easier for a skein (group) of geese to fly long distances. Studies on bar-head geese show that a group can fly 70% further than individuals. If you followed a skein of geese, you would see that every so often the goose at the apex is replaced and drops to the end of one arm of the group. This gives every goose a shot at the harder job of being the leader, and everyone a chance to be a follower.

What little jobs and tasks could you rotate among your people? Can people take turns at leading the team meeting or presenting the team figures, for example?

Think of the benefits. There will be less strain on you as you share the load, and you will have more time to manage people. Your people become multi-skilled. You can test them in management roles without committing to promotion. You give the ambitious a chance to shine, and you help everyone (including yourself) become more accustomed and comfortable with change. You also get to fly south for the winter. (No, sorry, that last one's a joke!)

The honking, by the way, is the geese's method of providing encouragement to each other and assuring themselves that they are all here and following. Those geese make a great team!

Think goose!

7.4

Set objectives that stretch people

In Secret 3.3 you were encouraged to set SMART objectives. Many companies put a C in front of the mnemonic – CSMART – whereby the C stands for 'challenging'. If an objective isn't challenging, it is, by default, easy, and thus might become boring very quickly. Being bored is a demotivator.

One challenging objective for you is to set and agree challenging objectives for your people! You need to provide enough challenge to make people want to achieve the objectives, but not so much challenge that people see them as impossible.

People with a high desire for attainment actively seek realistically challenging objectives that will test and prove their ability, thus justifying their advancement. These people are therefore relatively easy to agree challenging objectives with.

People with a fear of failure accept only objectives that they feel confident they can achieve – in other words, not very challenging objectives. These people present a challenge to you personally, as you have to find a way to get them to agree to more stretching objectives in order to improve their performance and confidence.

According to some theorists, there is evidence that some people with a morbid fear of failure will actively seek impossible challenges! Bizarre though this may sound, it allows them ultimately to justify their inevitable failure by blaming it on environmental factors, or even on you. These people present an even greater challenge to you.

How to manage people's resistance to challenge

1 Link the achievement of a challenging objective to the fulfilment of a personal motivator for that individual. This way the objective isn't simply their work goal; it will trigger a specific 'reward' which the individual wants. This can be a positive want: "When you have achieved this, you will be able to change your working hours to fit in better with childcare." Or it can be a 'pain avoidance' want: "When you have achieved this, you won't need to do the status reports that you hate!"

2 Break down a challenging objective into easier milestones that will be reviewed regularly. This way the person will be able to build up their confidence incrementally rather than working for a longer period with a risk of failure at the end. It allows them more control over their own levels of success and helps them sort the things they are good at from the bits they find difficult.

3 Set objectives that don't rely on factors outside the person's control. Activity and effort are indicative of skill and will, but don't necessarily lead to success. In a sales role, for example, objectives relating to calls made, customer footfall, flyers delivered and prospect enquiries are within the control of the sales person, whereas the actual buying decision is outside their control.

Set the right level of challenge for each individual.

7.5

Remember to develop yourself

Logically speaking, you are a team member in your boss's team, so your boss should be setting you stretching objectives and developing you. But don't rely on that! You need to ensure that you give yourself opportunities to develop, too.

In Secret 7.1 you learned that if you don't develop the people in your team, they might assume that's because you're scared they might then take your job, or even become your boss. This assumption is sometimes correct – some managers do deliberately keep their people down in order to maintain the status quo, and keep their position.

■ **Avoid 'Red Queen Syndrome'.** Some managers assume that, having become a manager already, they have nothing left to learn. These managers will be caught out by 'Red Queen Syndrome'. In Lewis Carroll's book *Through The Looking-Glass*, the Red Queen points out that you have to keep running just to stay in the same place. By analogy, the corporate environment keeps changing, and if you don't keep moving forward, you effectively fall back. Everyone around you is developing all the time, gaining in experience and expectation. If you don't develop yourself, you effectively fall behind the others. To presume that

one minute wonder Each day take a minute to write about what you have learned that day. The discipline of reflecting on your day is in itself valuable. It will also help you to learn as well as to recognize the value of that learning. It will help you to verbalize your learning to pass on to others and will also clarify how much things change in the world of work.

you have reached the pinnacle of your abilities is to stagnate and therefore to do this any earlier than a year or two before retirement is to ask to be overtaken.

■ **Don't fear the competition.** A manager who self-develops need not fear the employees catching up, because he or she is already ahead. It is possible that a member of your team is so brilliant that he or she overtakes you and becomes your boss, but you need not fear this either, because you can take credit for having recognized their potential! They will also respect you for having given them this chance, and will likely be a very good boss!

■ **Compile a 'learning log'.** Take time every week to make a record of what you have learned. This is called a 'learning log', and the discipline of completing it helps you to reflect, to grow, to learn and to understand yourself and others. The document or file itself becomes an invaluable aide memoir.

If you are not moving forward in the modern world, you are effectively moving backwards.

7.6

Improve the working environment

Assuming you are also responsible for the place and environment where your people work, you have the opportunity to develop the workplace itself.

Earnest Shackleton was putting together an Antarctic expedition in the early 1900s. He was short of funds and short of time. He allowed his men to decide what equipment to buy, how much of it to buy and how to pack it. This was unheard of in Victorian England. Uniquely the expedition returned with every man alive and in good health!

This story demonstrates that if you can get your people to think about their workplace and the way they do their work, then you will be able to unleash a very powerful force to improve your workplace, your team's processes, the methods they use and therefore their output. This is possible no matter what area you and your team work in, geographically or in terms of activity.

Get your team together. Tell them you want them to help you improve the areas shown opposite.

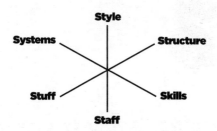

Six S star

■ **Systems.** Are the processes we use – e.g. filing, storage, IT, telephones – the best they could be?

■ **Style.** Is the trading or working style the best it could be? (Our image to our customers, peers, colleagues, competitors, the way we treat these people and each other.)

■ **Structure.** Is our organizational structure, including authorization, manpower and locations, the best it could be?

■ **Skills.** Does everyone have all the appropriate skills to do the job as best they can?

■ **Staff.** Do we have the right number of people in the right places?

■ **Stuff.** Do we have the best possible tools to fulfil our goals? Are the materials we use the best available?

By issuing a 'Six S' challenge like this you are bound to get some "No" answers. You can then ask people: "What would improve on what we have?" If their suggestions are ludicrously expensive, reply: "We can't afford that, so how could we do it for less?" You'll be amazed how inventive people are! If appropriate, group people into sub-teams to develop the ideas. If you've been following the earlier secrets in this book, you might set themes such as: "Empower! Delegate! Think Goose!"

Let your people take the initiative with ideas to improve the workplace.

7.7

Promote your people's image

Increasingly we live in the 'information age', in which everyone wants to know everything and everyone wants to tell. Certainly it is said that it isn't the best person who gets the job; it is the person who is best at getting noticed as being the best person. The same goes for your team.

There are two reasons to promote the image of yourself and your team. Firstly so that other people, such as bosses, customers, shareholders or voters, know that you are indispensable. Secondly so that the team knows that it is recognized.

Secret 4.1 explained what motivates human beings, and you can see that one aspect is the sense of belonging to a group. When your team is publicly recognized, you will have the pick of people wanting

case study A young manager in a rather staid organization bet his peers that he could get promoted within just six months. All of them took up his wager on the assumption that he was being naive. Over the next four months, he sent five senior managers a steady

to join, your existing people won't want to leave, and everyone will respect you as their leader.

■ Establish an award programme within the team, e.g. team member of the week/month/year. You then have some choices: you as the team leader can award the accolade; the team can vote for the winner; or you can really play the promotional angle and ask your customers to nominate the winner.

■ Send out a newsletter telling people what the team has achieved and is planning to achieve. This can be published online or on paper, and put up on appropriate bulletin boards, mailed out or just handed out.

■ You can send memos to senior managers commending certain individuals or actions for recognition and/or reward.

■ You can submit articles to the internal or external media about specific activities that are either finished, in midstream or at planning stage. These can become case studies for trainees or local business schools which then gives them longevity over a newsletter article.

■ You can offer yourself or a team member to speak at careers days, local community organizations or professional bodies.

■ You can set up a website or a web page to promote the activities of your team. It can include biographies and photos, case studies and details of who to contact for more information, services or joining opportunities.

If you don't 'blow your own trumpet', no-one else is going to blow it for you!

stream of memos praising his staff, recommending improvement opportunities, updating them on his team's achievements, and requesting them to come and speak to his team about strategic issues. He won the wager within five months.

Jargon buster

Acronym
An abbreviation formed from the initial letters or components in a phrase or name.

Action Centred Leadership
Model for leadership in which every decision and action taken should balance the needs of the task, the team and the individuals.

AIM
Acronym standing for Assess, Identify and Motivate – the three steps you need to take to recruit good people.

Customer footfall
The number of prospective customers who visit a site.

Delegation
Handing over tasks to other people. You must ensure that STAR principles apply to every task delegated (see opposite).

Direct reports
Staff who report directly to a particular posi~

~ ~eing paid but are not

Fire-fighting
In a business context, the term means the management of crises.

Followership
The act of following a leader.

Hawthorne effect
The well-known phenomenon that people's behaviour and output can change when they know they are being watched and measured.

Logo
A badge or symbol used by an organization as an identifying brand.

Matrix management
Where people are answerable to different managers on different teams. For instance, a project team that consists of a salesman, some logistics people, someone on accounts and someone from customer service, who are all managed by the project manager and other line managers at the same time.

Micro-management
Managing a person's work in too much detail, rather than setting up good motivating objectives and allowing the person to ~nage their own workload.

Milestones
Project management term for subsidiary objectives which must be achieved along the way to achievement of an ultimate goal.

Mnemonic
A word that spells out the initial letters of something we want to remember, for instance SMART.

PR
Public Relations – the way in which an organization or individual manages the image they have with external people.

Pyrrhic victory
A success where the objective is achieved but the cost is so great that the organization effectively ceases to function.

ROWE
Acronym standing for Results Orientated Work Environment – a model for a working environment that is orientated to recognizing and rewarding actual results rather than time spent doing something.

Situational Leadership
Model for leadership in which you alter your style of management according to the situation.

Synergy
(From the Greek syn-ergos, meaning working together.) The term used to describe a situation where different entities work together for a mutually beneficial outcome.

Sinecure
A 'job' that is not really a job at all but a title. Generally given to someone who cannot be found something of value to do.

SMART goal-setting
Acronym standing for Specific, Measurable, Achievable, Relevant and Timebound – the essential elements of a good objective.

STAR delegation
Acronym standing for Skill, Time, Authority and Responsibility – the four essential things needed when you delegate a task to someone.

Status quo
Continuing with the existing situation – not changing anything.

Team charter
Written guidelines setting out the behaviour expected of the team.

TOM principles
Acronym standing for Trust, Objectives and Motivation – the three principles of management.

Virtual team
A team that is scattered across different locations.

Further reading

Adair, John *Action Centred Leadership* (Gower, 1979) ISBN 978-0566021435

Adair, John *John Adair's 100 Greatest Ideas for Effective Leadership and Management* (Capstone, 2002) ISBN 978-1841121406

Belbin, R.M. *Management Teams: Why They Succeed or Fail* (Butterworth-Heinemann, 2010) ISBN 978-1856178075

Bennis, Warren G. and Nanus, Bert *Leadership: Strategies for Taking Charge* (Harper Business Essentials, 2003) ISBN 978-0060913366

Blanchard, Kenneth H. and others *Leadership and the One-Minute Manager* (HarperCollins Business, 2000) ISBN 978-0007103416

Deschamps, Jean-Philippe *Innovation Leaders: How Senior Executives Stimulate, Steer and Sustain Innovation* (John Wiley and Sons, 2008) ISBN 978-0470515242

Fisher, Kimball and Mareen *The Distance Manager: A Hands on Guide to Managing Off-Site Employees and Virtual Teams* (McGraw-Hill Professional, 2000) ISBN 978-0071360654

Holliforde, Sarah *The Motivation Handbook* (Chartered Institute of Personnel and Development, 2002) ISBN 978-0852929254

Lencioni, Patrick *The Five Dysfunctions of a Team* (Jossey-Bass, 2002) ISBN 978-0787960759

McGregor, Douglas *Leadership and Motivation* (MIT Press, 1966) ISBN 978-0262130233

Michaelson, Gerald A. *Sun Tzu: The Art of War for Managers – 50 Strategic Rules* (Adams Media, 2001) ISBN 978-1580624596

Morrell, Shackleton and Capparell *Shackleton's Way: Leadership Lessons from the Great Antarctic Explorer* (Penguin, 2002) ISBN 978-0142002360

Nelson, Robert B. *Empowering Employees through Delegation* (Longman Higher Education, 1994) ISBN 978-0786301997

Pincus, Marilyn *Managing Difficult People: A Survival Guide for Handling Any Employee* (Adams Media, 2005) ISBN 978-1593371869

On promoting your team

www.authenticpromotion.com/self-promo-tion/

http://37signals.com/svn/posts/741-ask-37signals-10-ways-to-get-ink

On team dynamics

www.belbin.com

Teambuilding exercises

www.businessballs.com

On branding your team

http://ries.typepad.com/ries_blog/2004/09/what_makes_a_go.html

Guides to leadership and followership

www.spangehawe.co.uk/duffersguides.htm

On motivation beyond money

www.myemployees.com/library/perception_realty.php

On the Hawthorne effect

www.envisionsoftware.com/articles/Hawthorne_Effect.html

The Leadership Alliance video

www.enterprisemedia.com/product/00017/leadership_alliance_short_cut.html

www.BusinessSecrets.net